St. Louis Community
College

Library

5801 Wilson Avenue
St. Louis, Missouri 63110

YALE STUDIES IN POLITICAL SCIENCE, 30

Rules and Racial Equality

EDWIN DORN

NEW HAVEN AND LONDON   YALE UNIVERSITY PRESS   1979

Designed by Thos. Whitridge
and set in Sabon type.
Printed in the United States of America by Edwards Brothers Inc., Ann Arbor, Mich. Published in Great Britain, Europe, Africa, and Asia (except Japan) by Yale University Press, Ltd., London. Distributed in Australia and New Zealand by Book & Film Services, Artarmon, N.S.W., Australia; and in Japan by Harper & Row, Publishers, Tokyo Office.

Library of Congress Cataloging in Publication Data

Dorn, Edwin.
  Rules and racial equality.

  (Yale studies in political science; 30)
  Includes index.
  1. Afro-Americans—Civil rights. 2. United States—Race relations. 3. Afro-Americans—Economic conditions.
I. Title II. Series.
E185.615.D65   301.45'19'6073   79–64228
ISBN 0–300–02362–6

To Franchelle

Contents

Tables and Figures

ix

Acknowledgments

THIS BOOK was a long time in the making. I would like to acknowledge some of the debts I accumulated along the way. My most constant adviser has been Douglas Rae. Doug introduced me to the rigorous study of inequality, offered detailed critiques of earlier drafts, and boosted me over quite a number of mental hurdles. I credit him with whatever analytic elegance is contained in the book.

Robert Dahl and Philip White offered considerable intellectual guidance and encouragement. They asked all the right questions; I hope they will find my answers satisfactory. John Fischer of *Harper's Magazine* was present at the very early stages and urged me to persevere. In ways too numerous to specify, the following friends also helped enormously: Chris Achen, Ted and Betsy Eismeier, Peter Geissler, Jennifer Hochschild, Olivia Surratt, and Paolo Zannoni.

Since coming to Washington, I have learned to appreciate the huge gap between "theory," such as presented in these pages, and practical programs. Mary Berry, assistant secretary for education, and Arthur Flemming, chairman of the Commission on Civil Rights, offered valuable lessons on this point. Dr. Flemming spent several hours discussing with me the programmatic implications of the book. I hope to explore those implications in later work.

For financial support I am grateful to the Southern Fellowship Fund and the Worthing Foundation, both of which exist to help minority scholars. I also wish to thank Mary Garrett, Susan Mudge, and Rendy Billings, who typed various versions of the manuscript. Marian Neal Ash of Yale Press provided what one expects of a good editor: sound advice, good humor, and studied impatience.

I owe profoundest gratitude to two remarkable women. My aunt and guardian, Miss Amy Groce, guided my childhood

with love and gentle wisdom. She gave me the will to succeed
and the courage to fail. My wife and favorite person, Franchelle
Stewart Dorn, helped me through the daily traumas of
preparing the book. Fran's career provided us an opportunity
to escape the drab Calvinism of New England and spend many
beautiful months in San Francisco. Aside from offering love
and pleasant diversion, Fran applied her considerable intelligence to helping me make the book more readable. I dedicate it
to her.

I

Introduction:
Open and Closed Rules

THIS BOOK is about rules and racial equality. The relationship
between the two is important, because the United States has
used rules to affect the distribution of goods[1] between the
races. Rules permitting or requiring racial discrimination have
had the effect of relegating blacks to second-class citizenship
with respect to rights and have also affected the ability of
blacks to compete for substantive rewards. Blacks were kept
from receiving certain types of training, were excluded from
certain jobs, and were paid less than whites for equal work.

With respect to the distribution of goods between the races,
the relationship between rules and results has long been regarded as *closed*. (A closed rule states or implies a substantive
result.) It is conventional wisdom that racial discrimination,
that is, rules permitting unequal treatment, produced substantive inequality. If blacks were not allowed to compete equally
with whites in the job market their incomes would be smaller.
If they were not allowed to sit on juries, it stood to reason,
given the prejudices of their white "peers," that blacks accused
of crimes would find the scales of justice weighing heavily
against them. If blacks were not allowed to vote, it was axiom-
atic that they would exert very little influence on public policy, save in the perverse sense that their presence in large numbers might incite whites to demand even more discriminatory

1. At this stage of the exposition, the term "goods" will be used in a
general sense to mean anything that is widely valued in the society. It
therefore connotes substantive goods such as income and wealth,
rights such as that of suffrage, and prestige or status. Later I will distinguish among these various forms of goods; indeed, later exposition
will hinge on those distinctions.

rules.[2] And so on, with respect to property rights and capital accumulation, public accommodation rules and black geographic mobility.

Given what we believed to be the closed relationship between rules and results, the solution to the problem of substantive inequality between the races appeared straightforward: Change the rules. If unequal treatment produced unequal results, then equalizing treatment ought to equalize results. Gunnar Myrdal made this argument thirty years ago and it is still part of our conventional wisdom: If blacks were given their political and civil rights and fair opportunity, "there would no longer be a Negro problem."[3]

Myrdal's statement is partly tautological and partly causal, for "the Negro problem" was actually two problems. One was unequal treatment; the other was unequal results, that is, the depressed socioeconomic status of blacks. Obviously, if blacks were given political and civil rights and equal opportunity, the first problem would disappear by definition: Ending discrimination will end discrimination. The causal relationship between equal treatment (rules) and equal result (racial equality) is logically and empirically more problematic, but we have tended to accept it nonetheless: Equal rules will produce equal results.

Our belief in the closed nature of the relationship between rules and racial equality has had two related effects. First, we have tended to concentrate on rules. This was the thrust of the civil rights movement. Now equalizing rules may be a desirable end in itself. Anyone who recalls the manifestations of second-

2. V. O. Key, Jr., is noted for the argument that the drive to disenfranchise blacks was strongest in those counties where blacks were a majority of the population. See *Southern Politics in State and Nation* (New York: Vintage, 1969), pp. 539–50. Donald Matthews and James Prothro verified that there was a strong inverse relationship between the percentage of blacks in a county and the percentage of blacks registered to vote. See "Social and Economic Factors and Negro Voter Registration in the South," *American Political Science Review* 57 (March 1963): 24–44.

3. *An American Dilemma: The Negro Problem and American Democracy*, 2 vols. (New York: Harper and Row, 1944), 1:24.

class citizenship that were prominent until a decade ago will understand why this is so: blacks being intimidated from entering polling stations; blacks being barred from state universities. The reader can exercise his memory here, and he will recall not only the manifestations of unequal rules but also the violence with which change was resisted. It was only a short time ago, but also a long time ago. We forget how important it was, scarcely a decade past, that a black man be allowed to enter a voting booth and cast his one small vote. Equal rights were worth dying for.

But just as important were the socioeconomic effects that changes in the rules were expected to produce. If blacks were afforded training equal to that of whites, if they were allowed to compete equally with whites for jobs and housing and public office, if they were given equal pay for equal work, then we could expect the socioeconomic standing of blacks to improve. In time, we expected the distribution of goods between the races to become roughly equal. This was the meaning of the statement, used so frequently during the civil rights movement, that nondiscrimination would allow blacks to "enter the mainstream of American life."

The second effect of our belief in the closed relationship between rules and racial equality is this: When the gap between the races failed to close rapidly in the 1960s, we believed the rules were at fault. That is, we suspected that the new rules, which prescribed equal treatment, were being violated. We began to look for persisting discrimination, for institutional racism, and for socioeconomic and cultural factors that continued to disadvantage blacks. We had little trouble finding them.[4]

---

4. The literature is voluminous; the following are among the major pieces. On the persistence of discrimination, see Otis Dudley Duncan, "Inheritance of Poverty or Inheritance of Race?" in *On Understanding Poverty*, ed. Daniel Moynihan (New York: Basic Books, 1968); Stanley Masters, *Black-White Income Differentials* (New York: Academic Press, 1975); and Albert Wohlstetter and Sinclair Coleman, "Race Differences in Income," in *Racial Discrimination in Economic Life*, ed. Anthony H. Pascal (Lexington, Mass.: Lexington Books, 1972). The phrase "institutional racism" was popularized by Stokely

And having found them, we had a reasonable reaction, given our causal assumptions: Make the rules harder to violate, or make it easier for people to enforce them.

But the problem is this: It may be that the relationship between rules and racial equality is not closed but *open*. (An open rule implies no substantive result.) If that is the case, then equal rules could perpetuate racial inequality. And if we believe racial inequality to be undesirable, then perhaps we ought to focus on results rather than on rules.

In the next part of this chapter I shall discuss the two types of rules, open and closed, and suggest how they are tied to results. The discussion will be fairly general. In later chapters I shall explore in greater detail the relationship between rules (defined as public policy prescriptions) and substantive equality between the races.

First, however, let me make this clear: The object of my concern is inequality between the races as it is affected by certain rules. From this statement three things follow. First, it is conceivable that factors other than rules affect racial inequality. Two extreme possibilities are that the races are inherently unequal with respect to talent or intelligence and that blacks actually prefer to be hewers of wood and drawers of water. These possibilities do not interest me. Second, not all rules affect the races directly, although one could engage in protracted debate

---

Carmichael and Charles V. Hamilton, *Black Power: The Politics of Liberation in America* (New York: Random House, 1967). Background factors are discussed in the "culture of poverty" literature of the 1960s, for example, Michael Harrington, *The Other America* (Baltimore: Penguin, 1963). Background factors as they affect blacks are discussed in E. Franklin Frazier, *The Negro Family in the United States* (Chicago: University of Chicago Press, 1939), and Kenneth Clark, *Dark Ghetto: Dilemmas of Social Power* (New York: Harper and Row, 1965). Moynihan borrowed heavily from Frazier to produce his influential report on the Negro family. See Lee Rainwater and William Yancey, *The Moynihan Report and the Politics of Controversy* (Cambridge: MIT Press, 1967). James Coleman emphasized the relationship between background factors and black educational achievement in *Equality of Educational Opportunity* Washington: Government Printing Office, 1966).

over precisely which rules are most important. I have resolved this problem by selecting for examination some rules that are fairly explicitly tied to race—for example, laws against discrimination. Third, I must reiterate my concern with *racial* inequality. I shall explain in chapter 2 how this is different analytically and normatively from other forms of inequality. I shall also demonstrate that substantive inequality between the races persists and shows few signs of abating.

Let us divide the set of conceivable rules into two types—open and closed. The difference between them will be this: Closed rules imply a rather specific result or set of results. If this is so, two things follow. First, from the rule I can infer results, even if they are not stated explicitly. Second, from the results I can infer whether or not the rule has been followed (assuming I can eliminate other possible explanations for the same result). Open rules do not imply a result, save themselves. From this it follows that (1) given a rule, I cannot infer a result, and (2) given a result, I cannot infer compliance or noncompliance with a rule. (See the appendix for a formal exposition.)

Some examples: Suppose I write a law that says, "Every person over age 65 *will receive* social security benefits." This is a closed rule with respect to social security benefits. I know what every person over 65 will receive. And if I find someone over 65 who is not receiving benefits, I can infer that the rule has been violated. But suppose I reword that rule to read, "Every person over 65 *is eligible for* social security benefits." It then does not guarantee that he will receive them. And if he does not receive them I cannot infer that the rule has been violated. I can, of course, list violation as one of the possible explanations, along with the possibilities that he does not want the benefits and that he is unaware of his eligibility.

Now consider rules for children dividing a cake. If the rule says, "All children will receive an equal piece," I can predict results and infer violations. It is a closed rule. But consider a harder case, the rule of cut-and-choose. This rule stipulates the following procedure: One child divides the cake, and he will be the last one to choose a slice. Can we predict results from this rule? We can, but *if and only if* we make certain additional assumptions. If we assume that the children are rational egoists, we can predict that the cake will be divided into equal pieces. The reason is obvious. The cutter does not want to be left with the smallest piece, so he will cut the cake to maximize his gains. Given the rule of cut-and-choose, and the assumption of rational egoism, we can predict a result even though the result is not stated in the rule. On the other hand, if the children are not rational egoists we cannot predict an outcome. The point is this: The rule of cut-and-choose is actually an open one. This may not be obvious to parents who have watched their children employ the rule, since the result is almost always the same—equal pieces of cake. But the reason for this outcome is that the rule is accompanied by another condition—rational egoism. The condition is analytically distinct from the rule, and if it is absent the results of the rule are indeterminate.

A more pressing example is a rule that says an accused has a right to have counsel present during interrogation. If I see someone being subjected to heated questioning without benefit of counsel, what can I infer? Not very much. Certainly I could not infer, without considerable evidence, that the rule was being violated. A safer inference—still subject to empirical verification, of course—is that he cannot afford a lawyer. The rule is open with respect to the actual presence of counsel. If the purpose of the rule is to protect the defendant's rights, something more is necessary. Two possibilities spring to mind. One is to replace the rule by one that is closed, one that *requires* that counsel be present. Another possibility is to supplement the present rule by conditions rendering it more likely that counsel be present. For example, I could stipulate that an accused who asks for counsel must be provided one, regardless of ability to pay. Notice that in the latter case the rule is still open. All I have done is to add a condition that facilitates enforcement or use.

Two points must be clarified. First, rules are not simply open or closed; rather, they are open or closed with respect to some specified result or set of results. Every rule is closed with respect to itself. The earlier example about social security eligibility is closed with respect to eligibility. But it is open with respect to the actual distribution of social security benefits. Likewise, a rule giving a certain person or group the right to vote is closed with respect to the right of named beneficiaries to vote. But it is open with respect to actual voting and to the substantive value of the vote.

The distinction between open and closed rules would be inconsequential save for this: We should know whether current and proposed rules will achieve certain desired results. If they are open with respect to desired results, then they are insufficient.

Second, openness is not synonymous with vagueness or ambiguity; and closedness is not synonymous with clarity or precision of meaning. Many rules are, of course, difficult to interpret. This is often true of legislation, and we leave it to the courts to give precise meaning to unclear laws. It is also often true of social conventions and philosophical ideals. Obviously, I cannot determine whether a rule is open or closed with respect to a specified result unless I have first defined the rule. Thus a considerable part of the book is concerned with developing clear meanings for the rules treated.

Two assertions allow me to connect the discussion of open and closed rules to the problem of racial inequality. First, a considerable amount of public policy consists of open rules. From the policy, nothing follows about the actual distribution of goods. This is especially true of those rules called rights. Given the statement, "Everybody has an equal right to x," nothing follows about whether everybody or anybody has x, or a certain amount of x[5]. All that follows is that if anyone has a right to x, "no one has either a greater or less right than he." Rights, then, provide a necessary but not a sufficient condition for the possession or exercise of x.

Consider suffrage. From the statement, "Everybody has a

5. This formulation is in Richard Wollheim, "Equality," in *Proceedings of the Aristotelian Society*, 56 (1955–56).

right to vote," nothing is implied about who will actually vote. Suppose that, in addition to the right, one must pay a poll tax. Or suppose the polling stations are open only from noon to four, when workers are not free to leave jobs; or that all polling stations are located in white neighborhoods where blacks feel unwelcome. In any of these cases, the right to vote will be exercised more frequently by some persons than by others.[6] Similar considerations lead us to expect that the right of private property and the right of free speech are open rather than closed.

Contrast the statement, "Everybody has an equal right to x," with the statement, "Everybody has a right to equal x."[7] From the latter, something follows about the distribution of x. This leads to the second assertion: Few rules in the United States are closed with respect to equal distribution. The United States is characterized by a liberal political economy, concerned with rules rather than with results. If the rule is considered fair, then the results, however unequal, are also considered fair. We pay relatively little attention to distribution and even less attention to the possibility of redistribution in the direction of greater substantive equality.[8] On the contrary, we have elaborate

---

6. Sidney Verba and Norman Nie, *Participation in America: Political Democracy and Social Equality* (New York: Harper and Row, 1972), especially chap. 10.

7. Wollheim, "Equality."

8. Public opinion polls are instructive on this point. Polls can be used in two ways. The most conventional use is to survey opinion on particular issues. But second, the contents of the polls—the questions asked—reveal a lot about the issues felt salient by the pollsters. By extension, I think it fair to say that polls reveal a society's agenda. If this is so then it is noteworthy that, since national opinion surveys began in 1937, fewer than a half dozen questions on national polls have asked about the redistribution of income and wealth. One can infer from this that the issue of redistribution is not prominent on our national agenda. There is a qualification: National polls have frequently asked about tax rates, social insurance programs, and efforts to alleviate poverty. But these issues are, at best, ancillary to more fundamental questions about redistribution. I wish to thank Jennifer Hochschild for this information, which she gleaned from an exhaustive study of national polls.

justifications for inequality among persons. (Unfortunately, arguments for inequality among persons are frequently extended so that they also justify inequality between the races. I shall show in chapter 2 that the leap from inequality among persons to inequality between racial groups involves a logical fallacy and often borders on sophistry.) The American view of equality is of a special sort; it looks to equality of rules, not to equality of results.

It is abundantly clear that race policy in the United States has tended to concentrate on rights. In progressive periods the tendency has been toward equalizing rights. But rights are open rather than closed rules. The only thing that follows from the fact that blacks and whites have equal rights is that blacks and whites have equal rights. Nothing follows about the exercise of rights or about the distribution of other goods. Not only that; it is often difficult to know when a right, per se, is violated. Since factors other than sheer repression may intercede between a right and its exercise, proving that a right has been violated is often problematical.

For example, if blacks owned no property we could not thereby infer that their rights to property had been violated. It may be that they simply cannot afford property. It may also be that whites who own property make it difficult for blacks to buy. Now if whites have covenanted to refuse to sell property to blacks, we know that they are indeed engaged in a violation of rights; or so we have known since restrictive covenants were outlawed thirty years ago.[9] But there are other tactics that do not constitute violation of rights but are very effective in keeping blacks from obtaining property. They include private sale, no-growth policies, and zoning regulations that restrict property acquisition to the very wealthy.[10]

9. The landmark case on restrictive covenants is *Shelly* v. *Kraemer*, 334 U.S. 1 (1948).
10. The Supreme Court has not yet spoken definitively on zoning and other policies that, in effect, serve to prevent blacks from building or buying homes in some areas. Since comprehensive guidance is lacking, lower court decisions vary from district to district. For a sum-

But let us not lose sight of the main point, which is that race policies tend to consist of open rules. Therefore, from rules about equal rights we can infer nothing about the distribution of goods. Equal treatment of the races under open rules need not produce substantive equality between the races. I use the phrase "need not" advisedly. Open rules may perpetuate inequality, or they may not. They may also be violated, and, since we cannot infer violation from result, proving violation of open rules requires that we observe process very carefully. In later chapters I shall examine two general sets of rules and their relationship to substantive racial equality. These are rules of suffrage and equal opportunity. I shall demonstrate that these rules actually serve to perpetuate substantive inequality between the races.

Let me state the plan of attack. I have already argued that the relationship between rules and racial inequality may be such that rules prescribing equal treatment will not produce substantive equality. Logically this is so because the rules regarding racial equality are open, and imply nothing about result. Whether it is actually so can be determined only by examining particular rules and their consequences.

Before I do that, however, I must establish, in chapter 2, that the races are actually unequal. That is not hard to do; but I will make a stronger claim—that the degree of substantive inequality between the races is not decreasing. The claims will be supported in part by conventional data on income and wealth. However, income and wealth are not the only forms of well-being that concern us. Others, such as status, political representation, control over resources, and the fate of those accused of crimes, must be considered. These are not as easily quantified as economic data, but they must be included in any responsible evaluation of inequality between the races.

---

mary of recent confusion, see Thomas I. Emerson et al., eds., *Political and Civil Rights in the United States*, vol. 2, 1975 Supplement (Boston: Little, Brown, and Co., 1975). pp. 236–42.

At all points of the analysis I shall try to inform the data with normative import, to show the reader why racial inequality ought to concern him. This will be accomplished by asking the reader to place himself behind a modified Rawlsian veil of ignorance. He will learn how the races fare but he will not know which race he is a member of.

In chapter 3 I shall examine rules of suffrage, which govern voting and political representation. I shall show that these rules are open, and then discuss a number of controversies that develop around efforts to cope with openness—controversies over political participation, white primaries, racial gerrymandering, and proportional racial representation. The general issues raised concern the value of suffrage to a recognizable, permanent, and disadvantaged minority. I shall show that we do not have a concept of political equality adequate to the conflicts likely to arise in a racially divided society.

Rules of suffrage govern the distribution of certain political goods. In chapter 4 I shall examine a rule that affects the distribution of economic goods. That rule is equal opportunity. My argument will be that equal opportunity will produce substantive equality between racial groups only under narrow conditions. One of these conditions is that the groups be roughly equal at the time the rule is imposed.

Chapter 4 also provides an opportunity to address a bit of conventional wisdom based on an analogy drawn between blacks and white immigrants. The vulgar version is, "If the Irish and Jews and Italians succeeded in America without receiving special treatment, then so can the blacks." I shall show that this type of thinking is the wrongheaded but perhaps understandable result of a biased perspective.

The concluding chapter will emphasize the messages contained in the body of the book: The rules examined will not accomplish what I believe we ought to be striving toward—substantive equality between the races. If we are to achieve this goal, we must be prepared to introduce different rules, which means we must confront some rather hard choices.

The book is modest by design. I do not offer an encyclopedic analysis, although my approach will provide a framework for analyzing more specific issues. In fact, I shall use it to look at racial gerrymandering, affirmative action, and several other controversies. Nor do I attempt to offer specific solutions, although some will be implied. What I offer is a new and elegant way of looking at an old and persisting problem.

2

Results: Substantive Inequality between the Races

INEQUALITY, when it exists, must be justified. Failure to do so produces "quarrels and complaints."[1] In this chapter I shall show that there is inequality between the races and that it cannot be justified.

Four things are necessary here. First, I need some method to help both the reader and the author avoid special pleading based on racial identification. Second, I need to provide analytic criteria for evaluating data on the distribution of goods between the races. These criteria are designed to answer the questions, "How do I recognize inequality?" and "How do I know when it has increased or decreased?" Third, I must provide the data. These include measures of economic well-being, political representation, and social status. Fourth, I will present and criticize some current justifications for racial inequality.

THE VEIL OF IGNORANCE AND CONSIDERATIONS OF RACE

Race has a singular influence on life in the United States. It has affected our constitutional structure, the nature of political conflicts, the distribution of economic and social status.[2] It

1. Aristotle, *Nichomachean Ethics*, trans. D. P. Chase (New York: E.P. Dutton, 1911), Book V: Justice.
2. Alexis de Tocqueville predicted that great differences between blacks and whites would persist long after slavery was eliminated. See *Democracy in America*, 2 vols., trans. Henry Reeve, rev. Francis Bowen, ed. Phillips Bradley (New York: Vintage, 1945). See vol. 1, chap. 18, for a discussion of the three races of North America. Robert Dahl asserts that "the tension between the effort to maintain a demo-

causes us to feel comfortable in some environments and uncomfortable in others, influences where we live and the types of music we prefer; it informs whom we vote for and the types of policies we want officials to pursue.

In short, race affects our interests. And where personal interest enters, detachment becomes difficult. But in order to evaluate racial inequality, some degree of detachment is desirable. Otherwise, the evaluations we make are likely to depend heavily on our racial self-interest. During the following analysis I ask the reader to detach himself from racial self-interest by pretending he does not know whether he is black or white. One way to do this is to join with other representative persons behind a veil of ignorance. Persons behind the veil are not told which race they belong to, nor can they guess.

I am borrowing the veil of ignorance from John Rawls, who used it as a vehicle to explicate a theory of justice.[3] However, where Rawls is concerned with the distribution of goods among persons, I am concerned with the distribution of goods among categorical groups.[4] Categorical groups are those in which the identity of the individual is fixed involuntarily and immutably. Specific categorical groups will vary across societies. In some places they are based on religion; in others they are based on language. Where there is little economic or social mobility, they may be based on class. In the United States, races are categorical groups.[5]

---

cratic republic and yet deny equality to Afro-Americans has dominated political life in this country from the Constitutional Convention to the present day. See *Democracy in the United States: Promise and Performance*, 2d ed. (Chicago: Rand McNally, 1973). See also William E. Burghardt DuBois, *The Souls of Black Folk* (New York: Signet, 1969); and Myrdal, *An American Dilemma*.

3. John Rawls, *A Theory of Justice* (Cambridge: Harvard University Press, 1971).

4. See Vernon Van Dyke's critique of Rawls, "Justice as Fairness: For Groups?" *American Political Science Review* 69 (June 1975): 607–14.

5. I shall not attempt to offer a more refined definition of categorical group. However, the way we look at groups clearly needs some

Rawls's representative men are placed behind a veil in order to deprive them of detailed knowledge about the world. They have general knowledge—they know that society is stratified and that talents are unequally distributed—but they do not know how they will fare once the veil is lifted. They do not know whether they will be rich or poor, dull or gifted. This ignorance precludes special pleading based on *informed* self-interest.

I propose to alter Rawls's device by injecting considerations of race. I do this in order to answer two questions. First, will race become a major factor in judgments about the distribution of goods? In order to answer the question, I will have to provide my representative persons with considerably more information than Rawls provides his representative men. They must be provided a framework for analyzing inequality between groups. They must be provided data. Finally, they must be presented some current justifications for racial inequality so they can judge whether those justifications are acceptable.

Second, will what they learn about race affect their view of the rules used for distributing goods? Here again I diverge from Rawls's scenario. Rawls's representative men begin *tabula rasa* and are asked to design a system of rules. By contrast, I shall ask my representative persons to evaluate an existing set of rules. It is the evaluation of rules that forms the core of this book.

---

refinement. For example, the identity "black" is fairly firmly fixed both within a generation and across generations. The same is true of castes. Sexes may also be considered categorical groups; discounting sex-change operations, a person born to one sex will remain of that sex. Further, the ratio of males to females remains fairly constant across generations. However, the ability of an individual to predict the sex of his or her offspring is very limited. A man who claims special privileges for his sex must recognize that his offspring may be disadvantaged by those claims. Thus while sexes may be regarded as categorical groups, they are different in at least two ways from races or castes or classes. First, no sex can act alone to preserve itself. Second, intergenerational predictability of sex identity is limited. These differences affect heavily the types of normative claims a sex-based group is able to make.

Suppose, for example, that we (as representative persons) decide that racial inequality exists and is unacceptable. We must then ask how existing rules affect the situation. The following possibilities exist. First, the rules may be closed with respect to the distribution of goods between the races so that we can predict their effects. If they will produce equality between the races, they will be acceptable. But if they will perpetuate or exacerbate inequality, then representative persons (RPs) will wish to change them.

Alternatively, the rules may be open; that is, they may allow no inferences about prospects for racial equality. Openness would be a source of concern because RPs will want protection against the effects of racial assignment. They will probably wish to substitute for the open rule one that is closed in favor of racial equality. This expectation derives from two facts: race is an unalterable condition; and it is without any conceivable moral significance.

First however, this: Each of the many facts presented to RPs could influence deliberations. Without providing RPs specific facts about themselves, I could tell them about religion, sex, ethnicity, regionalism. How can I justify injecting considerations of race but omitting other factors?

First, I am simply more concerned with racial differences than with other differences. This analogous to saying that I am more interested in studying political parties than in studying Poland, and needs no greater justification. But a second justification can be made, based on worst case analysis. The egregious past mistreatment of blacks, combined with the effects of that mistreatment on their future condition, justify attention to blacks as a group in need of remediation. The general facts about this society's past make being black a rational source of anxiety for each RP.

Another reason is that injecting more groups would tend to make the analysis far messier. This is so partly because of the types of analytic devices used later in the book; it is easier to deal with two groups than with many. Finally, injecting more groups would require me to state very early the generalizability of the analysis. I am not prepared to do that, because considerable research is required to discover which groups are like blacks with respect to a key criterion of group membership. That criterion is intergenerational predictability of group membership.

More on this point: Because of curious but important legal and social conventions, blacks have a very high predictability of group affiliation across generations. My black grandfather could predict with certainty that his offspring would be black. Whether such high intergenerational predictability of membership applies to Catholics, Kansans, Chicanos, or truck drivers is an empirical question. This predictability has resulted from a tendency to overdefine the group "Negro." While the legal definition of Negro has varied from state to state, being assigned to the group has generally required only a minuscule proportion of "Negro blood." Whether my grandfather's (or grandmother's) childbearing partner had been white, Catholic, or Kansan, the children would have been Negro.[6]

At this point I ask the reader to place himself behind a veil of ignorance, where he will be joined by a number of others. He does not know his race or anything else about how he will fare once the veil is lifted: Nor does he know any specific facts about other RPs. Aside from preventing special pleading, the veil serves another important function: Since RPs are indistinguishable with respect to race, sex, and socioeconomic status, they are rendered equal.

ANALYZING INEQUALITY

Definition of Inequality
Define inequality as a situation of unreciprocated envy.
Operationally, this means that there is inequality between A

6. Pauli Murray, ed., *State Laws on Race and Color* (Cincinnati: Women's Division of Christian Service, Methodist Church, 1951). Arkansas: "Any person who has in his veins any Negro blood whatever." From the Texas Penal Code, 1911, art. 484, acts 1887, p. 37: "The term 'Negro' includes also a person of mixed blood descended from Negro ancestry from the third generation inclusive, though one member of each generation may have been a white person."

and B if B would trade places with A, but A would not trade places with B. But this is insufficient; as the definition stands it permits ambiguity and silliness. For example, would a bored housewife trade places with a neurotic actress? The housewife may envy the actress her fame and wealth, but not her neuroses. To avoid this confusion, we will apply the definition to aggregates of goods, so that it reads: There is inequality between A and B with respect to some good, x, if B would trade parcels of x with A, but A would not trade parcels of x with B.

Three more refinements will allow us to explore inequality between the races. First, we must be able to make explicit statements about inequality with respect to the distribution of a single, divisible good. Second, we need criteria for evaluating change over time. Finally, we need some way to discuss the distribution of a number of goods. The refinements follow.

Describing Inequality—Simple Form
Consider how we could describe the distribution of a single divisible good, such as income. We would probably start with a measure of central tendency, such as the median. When we compare the medians of groups we can sense whether, generally, one group is better off than another. However, measures of central tendency are insensitive to within-group distributions. A measure such as median income would not necessarily distinguish between the distribution in figure 1 and that in figure 2. In both cases, group A may be better off on average than group B. But clearly there are many A's at the bottom of the distribution described in figure 2 who would trade places with most B's.

To compensate for this insensitivity, measures of central tendency must be accompanied by measures of dispersion, such as the standard deviation, or measures of concentration, such as the Gini coefficient. But these measures tend to pull us in different directions: Medians allow direct comparisons *between* groups, but standard deviations and Gini coefficients redirect our attention to inequality *within* groups.

An alternative is to compare distributions at quantiles, that

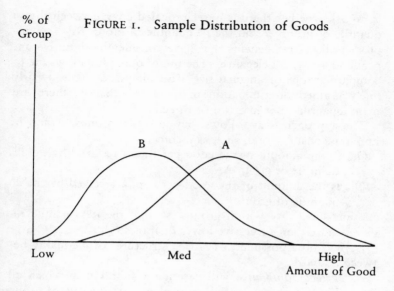

% of
Group

FIGURE 1. Sample Distribution of Goods

B   A

Low   Med   High
                              Amount of Good

FIGURE 2. Sample Distribution of Goods

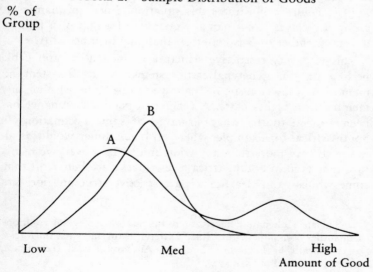

% of
Group

B
A

Low   Med   High
                              Amount of Good

is, to ask whether there is unreciprocated envy between the ith quantile of group A and the ith quantile of group B.[7] This approach allows refinements that have considerable intuitive appeal and analytical elegance. (The use of quantiles allows me to compare groups of unequal size. The analysis assumes a fairly finely grained discrimination of quantiles; that is, there are many quantiles, not just two or three.)

The approach is as follows: Suppose two groups, A and B, and one divisible good, such as income.

Q_{iA} is the amount of the good per capita received by the ith quantile of group A.

Q_{iB} is the amount of the good per capita received by the ith quantile of group B.

Assume inequality within groups, so that the nth quantile receives more than successive lower quantiles: $Q_{nA} > \ldots Q_{2A} > Q_{1A}$. It is now possible to describe structures of inequality between A and B.

1. *Perfect dominance* will describe a situation in which all quantiles of group A receive more than any quantile of group B. That is, group A is perfectly dominant over group B IFF $Q_{1A} > Q_{nB}$. Figure 3 illustrates this situation. Since no quantile of group B receives more than any quantile of group A, it follows that no member of B is better off than any member of A.

This is a very restrictive structure of inequality, applicable perhaps only in archetypal caste systems. In such a system, no member of a lower caste, B, is allowed to be better off than any member of a higher caste. A version of perfect dominance has been applied to the wage structure of some occupations in South Africa, for example, where no black miner would be allowed to earn more than any white miner. However, we recognize that even in South Africa a few blacks are better off than some whites. And clearly such a restrictive structure does not

7. Sinclair Coleman demonstrated the usefulness of distribution-by-quantiles comparisons in "Race Differences in Income," in *Racial Discrimination in Economic Life*, ed. Anthony Pascal (Lexington, Mass: Lexington Books, 1972).

FIGURE 3. Perfect Dominance

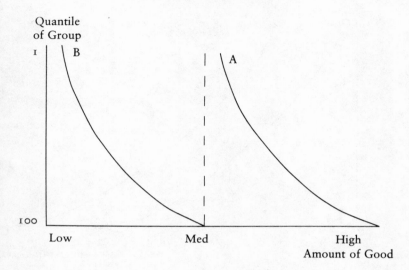

describe inequality between the races in the United States, where many whites may well envy some blacks.

2. *Strict dominance* is a criterion that recognizes some members of group B may be better off than average. We shall say that A is strictly dominant over B IFF $Q_{iA} > Q_{iB}$, $\forall Q_A$, $\forall Q_B$. This is to be read, "the ith quantile of A receives more than the ith quantile of B, for all quantiles of A and all quantiles of B." Figure 4 provides a graphic representation.

3. But it is possible to imagine a situation in which strict dominance does not apply. Consider the conventional wisdom (I wish to make no claims about its truth) about the socio-economic status of Japanese in the United States, which leads us to believe that they are concentrated in the middle income strata. If we are to contrast their situation with that of whites, who range from Rockefellers to dirt-poor Appalachians, we might find a distribution such as the one in figure 5.

In this situation, measures of central tendency would be misleading. The figure is drawn so that the lower quantiles of A

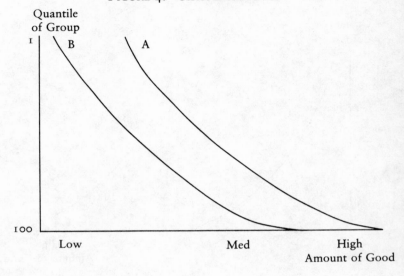

FIGURE 4. Strict Dominance

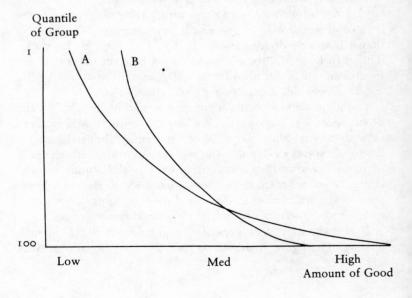

FIGURE 5. Qualified Dominance

(poor whites) envy the lower quantiles of B (lower-middle class Japanese), but upper quantiles of B envy upper quantiles of A. If it were to turn out that A had a higher average than B, we would say that there was *qualified dominance* in favor of A. Formally, qualified dominance means that group A is *on average* better off than group B IFF:

$$\sum_{i=1}^{n} Q_{iA} > \sum_{i=1}^{n} Q_{iB},$$

but for some quantile j, $Q_{jB} > Q_{jA}$.

Two points, one substantive, the other methodological: First, one can speculate that the structure of social conflict in a society is likely to be influenced by the structures of inequality just discussed. Where there is perfect dominance, conflicts over the distribution of goods are likely to be asymmetrical and disjoint. Public policy preferences will follow group lines, and there will be few distributive issues over which some members of one group will ally with members of the other. In other words, perfect dominance is likely to preclude crosscutting cleavages. Where there is strict dominance, some members of one group will have some policy interests in common with some members of the other group. In the United States, black Republicans are an example. Where there is qualified dominance, group affiliation will produce public policy agreement only on certain issues. For example, Japanese may be virtually unanimous on certain foreign policy issues, but their views on domestic policy may be influenced more heavily by socioeconomic factors than by categorical group membership.

Second, where perfect or strict dominance exists, measures of central tendency provide an adequate summary of differences between groups. With either of these structures of inequality, average differences may be read to suggest that there is unreciprocated envy at every quantile, Where qualified dominance exists, measures of central tendency may be insufficient or misleading. This is important because we wish our descriptions to be elegant and parsimonious. If measures of central tendency are sufficient to describe income differences between the races, we can avoid more obscure measures.

Describing Changes Over Time

Consider now how changes in a distribution should be described. I shall apply the same restrictions here as in the previous section—a single divisible good and two groups—and add one more: I shall assume that a measure of central tendency provides an adequate summary of the relative positions of the groups and of quantiles. That is, I assume at least strict dominance.

Figure 6 aids in examining the issues. The abscissa and ordinate plot the distribution of a good, y, between A and B. The following are denoted in figure 6:

1. *Perfect equality* between groups is a line through the origin with a slope of 1 (line OE), so that two conditions are satisfied:

    (a) The ratio of goods at the median is 1.

    (b) The absolute difference at the median is 0.

2. P marks the distribution between groups A and B at t_0; there is inequality in favor of A.

3. Line OR is the constant ratio line. Subsequent allocations to A and B that preserve the ratio at P will be at points along this line.

4. Line DD' is the line of constant difference. Subsequent allocations to A and B that preserve the absolute difference at P will lie along this line.

Suppose the total amount of y is changed. Any change will alter the distribution between A and B, so there will be movement from P to some other point. The question is this: Which directions of movement from P will lessen current inequality between A and B?

A rough answer is, any movement toward the line of perfect equality, OE. However, it is possible to be much more precise in characterizing the effects of specific directions of movement. One more restriction will simplify what follows. I shall consider only those movements that strictly satisfy the criterion of Pareto optimality. That is, I shall concentrate on those changes that (1) render at least one group better off, and (2) leave no group worse off. This means that if P were to be placed at the intersection of Cartesian coordinates, only those movements

FIGURE 6. Sample Inequality between A and B at t_0

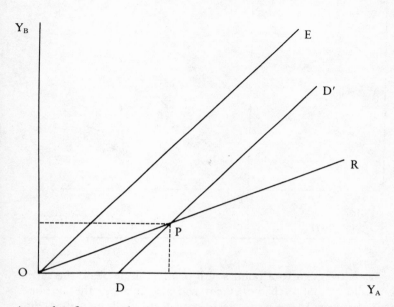

into the first quadrant are Pareto optimizing changes. (Such changes may not be Pareto equilibria if further changes are still possible.) The reader may check his bearings by glancing at figure 7.

I have already described the impact of movements along lines OR and DD', and the significance of line OE, the line of perfect equality. Now I shall describe other movements which satisfy the criterion of Pareto optimality.

1. Any movement to a point north of line PR (the segment of OR which lies in quadrant I) will move the ratio, Y_B/Y_A, toward 1.

2. Movement to a point north of PD' will decrease the absolute gap between Y_A and Y_B. Since line PD' is north of the constant ratio line, PR, it follows that such movement will also decrease the ratio. Therefore, movement north of PD' satisfies the conditions necessary to move toward equality between groups. Such movement will be called *equalization*.

FIGURE 7. Changes in Distribution between *A* and *B*

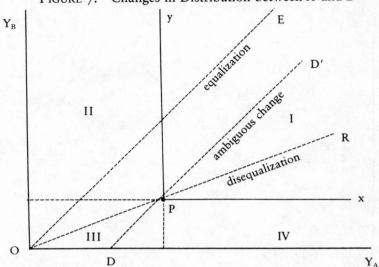

3. Movement to a point south of *PR* will decrease the ratio. It follows that such movement will also increase the absolute gap between *A* and *B*. Such movement will be called *disequalization*.

4. Movement into the region south of *PD'* but north of *PR* has the following effects: It moves the ratio toward *1*, but increases the absolute gap. Movement into this region will be called *ambiguous change*.

Describing Inequality—Complex Form

The analytic structure remains incomplete on two counts. First, it is obvious that many types of goods are distributed in a society—income, social status, political influence. We need some way to summarize the distribution of several types of goods. Second, the elegant devices just discussed are inappropriate for some goods. They are ideal for describing the distribution of highly divisible, easily measurable goods, such as income. But for other goods they constitute a kind of analytic overkill. These points imply the following: It is not possible simply to "add up" the distributions of different goods to produce a single measure susceptible of the fine distinctions made earlier. We need a way to characterize overall distributions that does not require or imply precise measurement.

Suppose that with respect to good x, A would trade places with B, but not vice versa; and with respect to good y, B would trade places with A, but not vice versa; and with respect to good z, A and B are indifferent over position. Two examples: First, consider inequalities between impoverished samurai and wealthy merchants in seventeenth-century Japan. Merchants no doubt envied the samurai their social status. And secretly the samurai probably envied the wealth of the merchants. (I say "secretly" because samurai codes disdained wealth obtained through trade.) Nineteenth-century England offers a more complex example—inequality between impoverished peers, wealthy merchants, and members of the middle class who had suffrage. With regard to social prestige, peers were envied. Merchants were envied for their wealth. And there was no envy across groups with respect to suffrage.[8]

When we find that envy runs in different directions according to the good being considered, we shall say that there exists a situation of *qualified inequality*. We will use the term *unqualified inequality* to describe a situation in which, for all goods considered, B envies A, but not vice versa. This terminology is necessary because it makes no sense to talk about "adding up" or "averaging out" inequalities in the distributions of several types of goods.

Summary

My goal was to devise criteria for analyzing the distribution of goods between primary groups. With respect to a single good that is easily measured and highly divisible, inequality can be

8. For convenience, I do not consider the effects of multiple balloting in England. Moliere's *Bourgeois Gentleman* parodies the presumptions of nobility and pretensions of the bourgeoisie in nineteenth-century France.

described with the terms perfect dominance, strict dominance, or qualified dominance. These terms apply to the existence of unreciprocated envy across quantiles.

Where perfect or strict dominance exists, measures of central tendency provide acceptable summaries of the degree of inequality between groups. Under conditions of perfect or strict dominance, medians can be used to analyze changes in a distribution over time. These changes can be described as equalization, disequalization, or ambiguous change. Since distributions of different types of goods cannot be "summed" on a single scale, the terms unqualified inequality or qualified inequality come into play.

Two caveats: First, data about the real world will often not fit neatly into the analytic framework, so the reader should anticipate some deviations from the fine distinctions drawn here. Second, my treatment of inequality between the races will not answer all conceivable objections. For example, we will still be speechless in the face of a statement such as, "But you people are so good at football!" However, I hope that the devices I have constructed will expose the silliness of such objections.

THE DATA

Income

Data on income indicate the following. First, there is strict dominance in favor of whites; at every quantile whites are better off. Figure 8 divides the distribution into five quantiles, each quantile representing 20 percent of the population. The results are quite clear. Table 1 shows the same result at selected percentiles. For example, the twentieth percentile of whites earns more than the fortieth percentile of blacks ($7,430 and $7,364, respectively, in 1975).

Second, change in the distribution over time has been ambiguous. (Since income inequality takes the form of strict dominance, medians are acceptable for summarizing changes.) Table 2 records changes in the ratio and the absolute gap at the me-

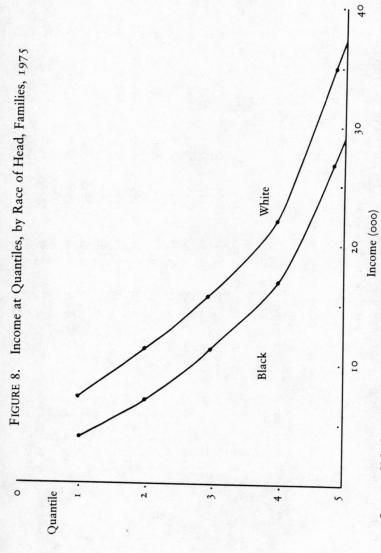

FIGURE 8. Income at Quantiles, by Race of Head, Families, 1975

Source: U.S. Census Bureau, *Current Population Reports*, P-60, No. 105, "Consumer Income," table 13.

TABLE 1. Income at Selected Positions, 1970–1975, Received by Each Fifth and Top Five Percent of Families, by Race of Head
(Current Dollars)

Income at Selected Positions

Year	Twentieth Percentile		Fortieth Percentile		Sixtieth Percentile		Eightieth Percentile		Top 5 Percent	
	White	Black and Other	White	Black and Other	White	Black and Other	White	Black and Other	White	Black and Other
1950	1836	723	3025	1479	3961	2254	5502	3178	8877	5200
1951	2154	827	3368	1625	4370	2458	5944	3577	9339	5568
1952	2282	1122	3559	1945	4708	2733	6325	3622	9793	6019
1953	2354	1038	3824	2033	5048	2992	6778	4378	10495	7117
1954	2235	929	3741	1848	4984	2990	6796	4183	10703	6685
1955	2465	1043	4005	2013	5306	3129	7104	4423	10917	6733
1956	2729	1092	4324	2127	5698	3213	7638	4661	11874	7340
1957	2813	1078	4467	2193	5829	3427	7747	5087	11854	7813
1958	2874	1169	4577	2172	5996	3433	7965	5033	12500	8141
1959	3000	1207	4872	2180	6300	3567	8600	5300	13050	8722
1960	3025	1310	5000	2502	6585	3900	9000	6000	13964	9892
1961	3086	1421	5041	2474	6862	3952	9292	6000	15000	10268

1962	3300	1476	5281	2696	7040	4000	9800	5942	15159	10000
1963	3480	1674	5502	2787	7481	4200	10093	6400	15525	10376
1964	3586	1857	5800	3100	7800	4630	10500	7000	16056	11400
1965	3870	1927	6100	3300	8123	4900	11013	7300	17067	11800
1966	4270	2175	6700	3750	8924	5520	12000	8120	18514	12510
1967	4500	2340	7000	4011	9301	6000	12528	9000	19500	14076
1968	5000	2705	7640	4490	10097	6800	13700	10089	21000	15800
1969	5360	2959	8375	5000	11090	7356	15021	10920	23298	17238
1970	5500	2972	8727	5246	11691	7900	15929	11700	24941	18521
1971	5661	3062	9055	5390	12101	8000	16640	12248	27890	19411
1972	6124	3148	9815	5506	13224	8815	18158	13457	28500	20400
1973	6660	3510	10599	6050	14400	9376	19816	14050	30645	23000
1974	7205	3859	11400	6736	13500	10500	21188	16016	32966	24500
1975	7430	4100	12000	7364	16450	11358	22614	17017	35000	26600

Source: U.S., Department of Commerce, Bureau of the Census, *Current Population Reports*, P-60, no. 105, "Consumer Income" (Washington: GPO, 1977), table 13.

dian from 1950 to 1977. Examination of table 2 reveals that the absolute gap has widened almost every year for the past quarter century. This is so whether one uses current or constant dollars, although the increase is less dramatic if one uses constant dollars. The ratio has shown some fluctuation. From .57 during the Korean War (1952), the ratio declined to a low of .51 during the recession of 1958, then improved throughout the 1960s, reaching a peak of .61 in 1969 and 1970. Since the absolute gap increased and the ratio closed slightly, we conclude that there was ambiguous change between 1950 and 1970. However, the 1970s represent a period of disequalization: by both ratio and absolute gap criteria, blacks were worse off in 1977, in comparison with whites, than they were at the end of the 1960s. Figure 9 offers graphic evidence of the trend.

I am not suggesting that blacks are, in an absolute sense, worse off now than during the Great Society. The U.S. economy has grown since the mid-1960s, and blacks have benefited from that growth. However, to say that blacks are absolutely better off is not to say that they have improved their position vis-à-vis whites. The income data suggest a contrary conclusion. For the past quarter century, change in income inequality between the races has been ambiguous at best.

Now let me take issue with some of those who would disagree. In recent articles, RAND economists Finis Welch and James Smith have purported to show that blacks and whites are moving toward equality.[9] To be fair I should note that their research concerns only earnings, which is one type of income. But even in the narrow realm to which their research speaks, Welch and Smith have committed some serious errors.

First, they use ratios exclusively. They find that the ratio of black male earnings to white male earnings has improved over time—from .59 in 1947 to .73 in 1975—and conclude that the earnings of black and white men are moving toward equality. Had they instead looked at the absolute gap they might have al-

9. James P. Smith and Finis Welch, "Race Differences In Earnings: A Survey and New Evidence," Rand Corporation, 1978, prepared with the support of a grant from the National Science Foundation.

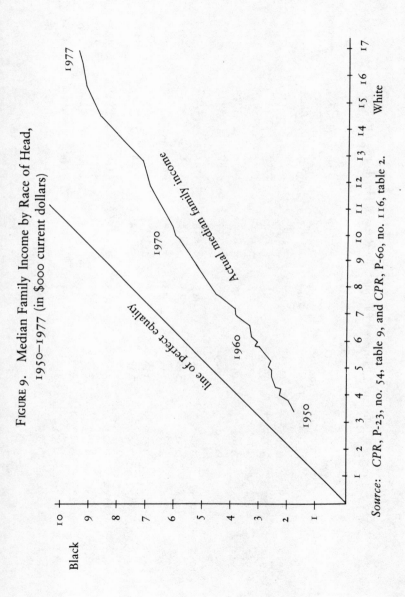

FIGURE 9. Median Family Income by Race of Head, 1950–1977 (in $000 current dollars)

line of perfect equality

Actual median family income

1950

1960

1970

1977

Black

White

Source: CPR, P-23, no. 54, table 9, and CPR, P-60, no. 116, table 2.

TABLE 2. Median Income of Families, by Race of Head, 1950 to 1977

Year	Current Income		Absolute Difference	Ratio	CPPI[b]	Constant Income (1967)		Constant Dollar Difference
	White	Black[a]				Whites	Blacks	
1950	3445	1869	1576	.54	1.387	4778	2592	2186
1951	3859	2032	1827	.53	1.285	4959	2611	2348
1952	4114	2338	1776	.57	1.258	5175	2941	2234
1953	4392	2461	1931	.56	1.248	5481	3071	2410
1954	4339	2410	1929	.56	1.242	5389	2993	2396
1955	4605	2549	2056	.55	1.247	5742	3178	2564
1956	4993	2628	2365	.53	1.229	6136	3230	2906
1957	5166	2764	2402	.54	1.186	6127	3278	2849
1958	5300	2711	2589	.51	1.155	6122	3131	2991
1959[a]	5893	7808	2846	.52	1.145	6748	3489	3259
1960	5835	3233	2602	.55	1.127	6576	3643	2933
1961	5981	3191	2790	.53	1.116	6675	3561	3114
1962	6237	3330	2907	.53	1.104	6886	3676	3210
1963	6548	3465	3083	.53	1.091	7144	3780	3364
1964	6858	3724	3134	.54	1.076	7379	4007	3372

1965	7251	3886	3365	.54	1.058	7672	4111	3561
1966	7792	4507	3285	.58	1.029	8018	4638	3380
1967	8234	4875	3359	.59	1.000	8234	4875	3359
1968	8937	5360	3577	.60	.960	8580	5146	3434
1969	9784	5999	3785	.61	.911	8913	5465	3448
1970	10236	6279	3957	.61	.860	8803	5400	3403
1971	10672	6440	4232	.60	.824	8794	5306	3488
1972	11549	6864	4865	.59	.799	9228	5484	3744
1973	12595	7269	5326	.58	.752	9471	5466	4005
1974	13356	7808	5548	.58	.678	9055	5294	3761
1975	14268	8779	5489	.61	.621	8860	5452	3408
1976	15537	9242	6259	.59	.587	9120	5739	3381
1977	16740	9563	7177	.57	.554	9274	5298	3976

Source: U.S., Department of Commerce, Bureau of the Census, *Current Population Reports*, P-23, No. 54, "The Social and Economic Status of the Black Population of the United States, 1974" (Washington: GPO, 1975), table 9; CPR, P-60, No. 116, "Money Income and Poverty Status of Families and Persons in the United States, 1977" (Washington: GPO, 1978); I wish to thank Dwight Johnson of the Census Bureau for helping me locate the most recent data.

^a "Black" income prior to 1964 actually comprises "Negro and Other Races." An exception is 1959, when the Census Bureau measured black income separately.

^b The Consumer Purchasing Power Index (CPPI) is the inverse of the Consumer Price Index. It is obtained from *Statistical Abstract of the United States, 1977*, Table 759, p. 470. Current income times CPPI equals constant income.

tered their conclusions. The gap has grown from approximately $1,000 in 1947 to $3,000 in 1975.[10] In my view that change is not trivial, and no responsible analyst should overlook it. Welch and Smith, however, do not even allude to it.

An even more embarrassing oversight is the authors' failure to tell us that the number of working black males actually *declined* during the very period when the most dramatic ratio improvements occurred. From 1969 to 1975 the number of black male full-time workers declined by eight percent, while the number of white male full-time workers increased slightly.[11]

Welch and Smith do not tell us about declining black male employment, just as they do not tell us that the income gap between blacks and whites has increased. They omit facts that would contradict their optimistic assertions.

Wealth

Data on wealth are much harder to come by than data on income, especially in forms that allow direct comparison of the races. However, two sets of data offered below establish the following: At every income level, white wealth exceeds black. The studies cited below also offer important ancillary findings.

Figure 10 summarizes the results of the 1967 Survey of Economic Opportunity. Figure 11 presents the results of a microeconomic study of home ownership in one city. Since home ownership is the major form of wealth holding for most families, these data are especially revealing. The differences shown in figure 11 become even more dramatic when one considers that blacks and whites have different rates of home ownership. In 1973 only 43 percent of black households lived in

10. Welch and Smith do not print the source of their data, save to mention that it is from the Census Bureau. As best I can determine, their data came from the *Current Population Reports*, Series P-60, various editions, especially no. 69, tables A-7 and A-8 (1970); no. 80, table 59; no. 85, table 59; no. 90, table 61; no. 97, table 68; no. 101, table 68; and no. 105, table 56.
11. Robert B. Hill, *The Illusion of Black Progress* (Washington: National Urban League, 1978), pp. 16–18 and table 10.

homes they owned or were buying. The comparable figure for whites was 67 percent. Further, the rate of black home ownership remained constant in the early 1970s, while the rate of white home ownership increased.[12]

Inequality in the distribution of wealth is greater than inequality in the distribution of income. "On average black families have less than one-fifth the total wealth accumulation of white families."[13] Figures 10 and 11 show that this inequality is not simply the result of skewing caused by the presence of very rich whites. Rather, a form of strict dominance applies: "Black families at each tabulated income level had less than one-half the wealth accumulation of white families in the same income bracket."[14]

An important related finding is that blacks and whites tend to hold wealth in different forms. Blacks usually hold no financial assets, while such assets (stocks, bonds) comprise a large portion of whites' portfolios. With respect to nonfinancial assets, "black families have a definite tendency toward accumulation in assets yielding consumption services (cars, trucks, housing) while whites hold a greater share of their financial wealth in income-providing assets (farms, other real estate, and business equity)."[15] The upshot of this difference in the form of wealth holding is that the wealth of whites appreciates considerably faster than the wealth of blacks, thus causing the gap to widen. We do not have data that allow us to chart changes in the distribution of wealth between the races over time. But what we know about differences in appreciation rates leads us to conjecture that changes have been ambiguous at best.

12. U.S., Department of Commerce, Bureau of the Census, *Current Population Reports* (CPR), P-23, no. 54, "The Social and Economic Characteristics of the Black Population, 1974" (Washington: Government Printing Office, 1975), p. 134.

13. Henry S. Terrell, "Wealth Accumulation of Black and White Families: The Empirical Evidence," *Journal of Finance* 26 (May 1971): 363–77.

14. Ibid.

15. Ibid.

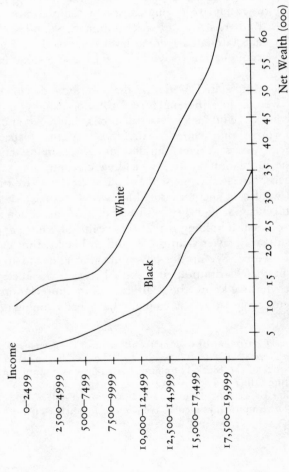

FIGURE 10. Net Wealth of Black and White Families in 1967 by Income Class (mean amounts in dollars)

Source: Henry Terrell, "Wealth of Black and White Families: The Empirical Evidence," *Journal of Finance,* 26: 363-77 (May 1971).

FIGURE 11. Estimated Value of Single-Family, Owner-Occupied Units for Black and White Owners, by Income

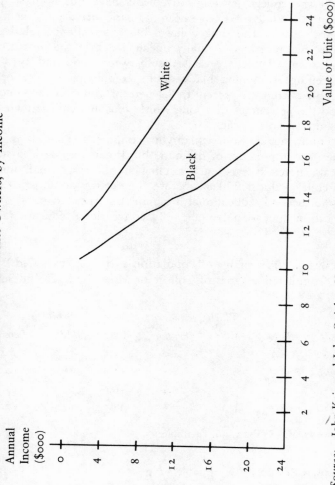

Annual
Income
($000)

Value of Unit ($000)

White

Black

Source: John Kain and John Quigley, *Housing Discrimination* (New York: Columbia University Press, 1975), p. 179.

Education

Inequality in educational attainment persists, although the gap appears to be closing at the elementary and secondary school levels. By 1974, 72 percent of blacks between the ages of twenty and twenty-four had completed high school. The comparable figure for whites is 85 percent.[16]

At the college level improvements have not been so pronounced. While there have been dramatic increases in the number of blacks attending college, black attendance relative to white has remained virtually unchanged over the past decade and a half. Table 3 reveals that between 1960 and 1974 the percentage of young black adults completing college nearly doubled, from 4.1 percent to 8.1 percent. But over the same period the percentage of young whites finishing college increased by almost 90 percent.

Following are some qualifying comments: First, it is clear that our impression of dramatic black gains is partly a statistical artifact. It is as much a statement about the small number of college-educated blacks before 1960 as it is about gains since 1960. Second, educational attainment statistics conceal differences in educational quality. By conventional educational at-

TABLE 3. Percentage of Population 25 to 34 Years Old Who Completed 4 Years of College or More, by Race and Sex

| | | Black | | | White | |
Year	Total	Male	Female	Total	Male	Female
1960	4.1	4.1	4.0	11.9	15.8	8.3
1966	5.7	5.2	6.1	14.6	18.9	10.4
1970	6.1	5.8	6.4	16.6	20.9	12.3
1974	8.1	8.8	7.6	21.0	24.9	17.2

Source: CPR, P-23, no. 54, table 68.

16. CPR, P-23, no. 54, table 67, p. 97.

tainment criteria, black high school graduates "know less" than their cohorts. Regardless of the reasons for differences in scores on achievement tests, those differences affect future employment and educational opportunities.[17] Further, there is evidence that blacks who receive post-secondary education tend disproportionately to take it at less selective four-year colleges, junior colleges, and trade schools.[18] Again, regardless of the reasons for this tendency, it places blacks at a competitive disadvantage.

With respect to graduate and professional training: In 1972, 2.7 percent of blacks and 8.5 percent of whites had completed at least one year of graduate work.[19] For the past few years the percentage of black and white college graduates who go on to advanced training has been about the same—one-third. But blacks must rely much more heavily on scholarships and borrowing to attend graduate and professional schools. Only 33 percent of blacks were able to pursue advanced courses without borrowing; 62 percent of whites were able to avoid going into debt.[20] Given recent challenges to affirmative action programs in professional schools and major cutbacks in fellowship aid to minorities, it is not likely that blacks will soon close the gap in graduate and professional training. Indeed, the gap may begin to widen.

17.   See generally, James Coleman, *Equality of Educational Opportunity* (Washington: GPO, 1966); Christopher Jencks et al., *Inequality: A Reassessment of the Effects of Family and Schooling in America* (New York: Basic Books, 1972); and James Rosenbaum, *Making Inequality: The Hidden Curriculum of High School Tracking* (New York: John Wiley & Sons, 1976).

18.   Alexander W. Astin, "The Myth of Equal Access in Public Higher Education," cited in Ernest Holsendolph, "Black Presence Grows in Higher Education," *New York Times*, November 14, 1976, p. 15.

19.   Holsendolph, "Black Presence."

20.   Leonard Baird, "A Portrait of Blacks in Graduate Studies," presentation before House Committee on Education and Labor, *Hearings on Student Financial Assistance*, 93d Cong., 1st sess., 1974, 14:67–71.

Unemployment

Figure 12 compares black and white unemployment rates from 1960 to 1977. Two things are clear. First, the unemployment rate for blacks is considerably higher than that for whites at every point in the series. Second, black and white unemployment rates vary in the same direction; as white unemployment increases, so does black. Civil rights acts and affirmative action programs appear to have had little impact on relative unemployment rates. Figure 13 indicates that the black unemployment rate is consistently twice that of whites.

But the official unemployment rate, distressing as it is, conceals two crucial points. First, the official statistics probably understate the true extent of unemployment among blacks. The Bureau of Labor Statistics counts as unemployed only those who are not working but are still actively looking for work. It excludes those who have given up searching for a job. The Urban League argues that if those "hidden unemployed" were counted, the black unemployment rate would be upwards of 20 percent, growing to 50 percent in inner city poverty areas.[21] Anyone passing through an inner city ghetto on a weekday afternoon has seen them. They are the women on the stoops of Harlem. They are the men on The Hill in New Haven. They are the hopeless shells leaning against decaying storefronts in Houston's Fifth Ward. We have all seen them, but to the government statistician they are conveniently invisible. They have been undertrained by our educational system, maligned by middle-American rhetoric, and finally rendered irrelevant by benign neglect.

A second point has to do with the identity of the unemployed. Unemployment is highest among those who have left school recently. The official unemployment rate among blacks aged 16 to 19 has been 35 to 40 percent for the past three years, compared with 16 percent for whites in the same age

21. Robert B. Hill, *Special Policy Report: Black Families in the 1974–75 Depression* (Washington: National Urban League, 1975). The Census Bureau attempts to count the "hidden unemployed" by asking the unemployed why they are not working.

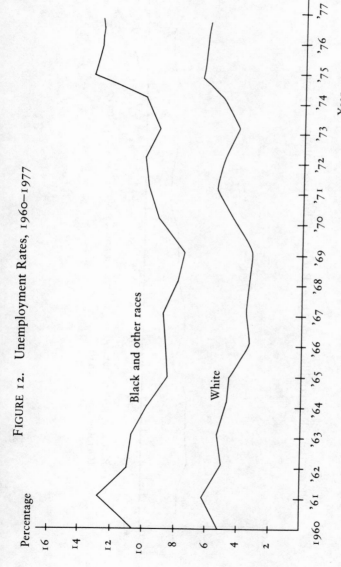

FIGURE 12. Unemployment Rates, 1960–1977

Black and other races

White

Percentage

16
14
12
10
8
6
4
2

1960 '61 '62 '63 '64 '65 '66 '67 '68 '69 '70 '71 '72 '73 '74 '75 '76 '77

Year

Source: U.S. Department of Labor, Bureau of Labor Statistics, "Employment and Earnings," Vol. 24, No. 10 (October 1977), chart 11.

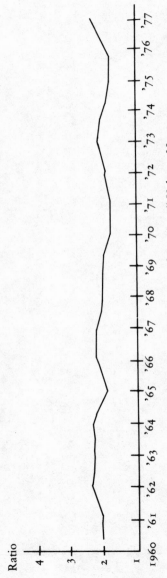

FIGURE 13. Ratio of Black and Other Races to White Unemployment, 1960–1977

Source: Bureau of Labor Statistics, "Employment and Earnings," Vol. 24, No. 10 (October 1977), Chart 11.

group.[22] What this means is that our society is in danger of producing in the next adult generation a large population of blacks who have never held a job. And the longer they remain unemployed, the smaller are their changes for securing permanent employment. A teenager leaving high school is willing to accept menial work; he has hope for advancement. A twenty-five-year-old is likely to find menial work demeaning and unfulfilling. One's skills may not increase as one grows older, but one's expectations, pride, and real needs will grow. Further, employers are willing to hire young people who have no work experience, but adults without work experience will not be regarded sympathetically.

The upshot is that large numbers of young black adults are chronically unemployed and dependent, and the weight of their condition increases with each passing year. Because their skills and work experience are not commensurate with their age, their condition is likely to be unchanged even if there is a general improvement in employment rates.

Social Status

The social status of a group is analytically distinct from its economic status. Earlier I offered European aristocrats and Japanese samurai as historical examples. A similar disjuncture of economic and social status occurs in the United States, based on the ascriptive characteristics of groups or on membership in particular occupations. Ministers, doctors, and teachers enjoy higher social prestige than politicans, entertainers, and oil field roughnecks even though, on average, members of the latter groups may be quite well off financially.

There are two conditions under which blacks might be considered equal or superior to whites in social status, despite their lower economic standing. First, blacks could be overrepresented in high-prestige (but modest-income) occupations. For example, if blacks were prominent on university faculties, the status of blacks as a group could be enhanced disproportion-

22. Bureau of Labor Statistics, vol. 24, no. 10, table A-35 (October 1977).

ately. Second, blacks could be envied because of some special value attached to being black. This valuation could be related to some special quality—beauty, intelligence, political acumen, physical prowess, gentility—or it might be a much more general, indefinable quality.

Two types of evidence will be used to inform this issue: (1) the actual representation of blacks in occupations; (2) how whites regard blacks.

1. Blacks are beginning to fill white-collar occupations previously closed to them. Tables 4 and 5 summarize these changes over time. The tables suggest a trend toward equality of occupational status. However, the data must be interpreted cautiously for the following reasons.

First, changes over time are difficult to interpret literally because the Census Bureau changes its occupational classifi-

TABLE 4.   Occupation of Employed Men, by Race, Selected Years
(in Thousands)

Occupation	1964		1970		1974	
	Black and Other Races	White	Black and Other Races	White	Black and Other Races	White
Total employed:						
thousands	4,359	41,114	4,803	44,157	5,179	47,349
percentage	100	100	100	100	100	100
White collar	16	41	22	43	24	42
Blue collar	58	46	60	46	57	46
Service workers	16	6	13	6	15	7
Farm workers	10	7	6	5	4	5

Source: CPR, P-23, no. 54, table 48, p. 73.

TABLE 5. Occupation of Employed Women, by Race, Selected
Years
(in Thousands)

Occupation	1964		1970		1974	
	Black and Other Races	White	Black and Other Races	White	Black and Other Races	White
Total employed:						
thousands	3,024	20,808	3,642	26,025	4,136	29,280
percentage	100	100	100	100	100	100
White collar	22	61	36	64	42	64
Blue collar	15	17	19	16	20	13
Service workers	56	19	43	19	37	19
Farm workers	6	3	2	2	1	2

Source: CPR, P-23, no. 54, table 49, p. 77.

cations from time to time.[23] Second, most of the gains have
been among lower level white-collar workers, especially wom-
en. From 1964 to 1974 there was a 20 percent increase in
the number of black female white-collar workers. But of this,
14 percent, or 70 percent of the total change, was in the category of clerical workers. Advancement within this category is
limited, as is promotion from this category to management
and professional work.

Third, even in those categories where advancement is not se-
verely limited, we have no basis for projecting that black white-
collar workers will advance as rapidly as their white cohorts. It
is possible that subtle and invidious forms of bias will continue
to impede the advancement of black professionals.

Fourth, increases in the ranks of black professionals will depend in part on educational qualifications. During the late

23. CPR, P-23, no. 54, note, p. 73.

1960s and early 1970s, special efforts were made to recruit blacks into graduate and professional schools and to provide them financial aid. Recently, recruitment efforts have come under court challenge, and fellowship aid for blacks has been reduced considerably.[24] The effects of these actions are already visible: minority enrollment has dropped in medical schools and has leveled off in law schools.[25] As summarized in table 6, despite encouraging gains, inequality of occupational status persists.

2. There was a time when whites were virtually unanimous in their belief that blacks were members of a distinctly different and inferior class of humanity, and therefore subject to a different standing in law and social status. Long after blacks were granted legal equality by the Civil War Amendments, black leaders such as Booker T. Washington felt obliged to assure whites that there would be no "agitation" for social equality between the races.

Obviously whites' opinions of blacks—and blacks' opinions of themselves—have changed. Today, advocates of white supremacy are curious (although dangerous) anachronisms. Very few whites continue to reject outright the principles of equal protection, or even the ideal of social and economic equality between the races. But a decline in overt racism does not necessarily mean that all whites view blacks as equals, or as equals in every respect. Whites may accept political equality in principle but refuse to vote for blacks running for office. Whites may accept the principle of equal housing opportunity, but react nega-

24. The best publicized challenges are *Defunis* v. *Odegaard*, 416 U.S. 312 (1974) on admissions policies at the University of Washington Law School; and *Regents of the University of California* v. *Bakke* , No. 76-811, June 28, 1978, on admissions policies at Cal-Davis Medical School.

25. Jan Hemming, "Fund Cuts Threaten Academic Minorities," *New Haven Register*, October 24, 1976, p. 1; Editorial, *New York Times*, November 21, 1976; and Robert L. Jacobson, "No Progress in Recruiting Minority Medical Students," *The Chronicle of Higher Education*, September 2, 1978.

TABLE 6.   Occupation of the Employed Population, by Race,
1974
(Annual Averages)

Occupation	Total (000)	Black (000)	White (000)	% Black of Total
Total employed	85,936	8,112	76,620	9
White-collar workers	41,738	2,309	38,761	6
Professional and technical	12,338	710	11,368	6
Managers and administrators, except farm	8,941	277	8,562	3
Sales workers	5,417	158	5,203	3
Clerical workers	15,043	1,102	13,629	8
Blue-collar workers	29,776	3,411	26,029	12
Craft and kindred workers	11,447	769	10,603	7
Operatives, except transportation	10,627	1,421	9,075	13
Transport equipment operatives	3,292	459	2,805	14
Nonfarm laborers	4,380	763	3,547	17
Service workers	11,373	2,130	9,037	19
Farm workers	3,048	225	2,793	7

Source: CPS, P-23, no. 54, table 50, p. 75.

tively to the imminent possibility of a black family moving in next door.

What are current white attitudes toward blacks?[26] First, al-

26. Charles S. Bullock, III, and Harrell Rodgers, Jr., *Racial Equality in America: In Search of an Unfulfilled Goal* (Pacific Palisades, Calif.: Goodyear Publishing Co., 1975). p. 155. For black attitudes, see ibid., chap. 6; and Howard Schuman and Shirley Hatchett, *Black Racial Attitudes: Trends and Complexities* (Ann Arbor, Mich.: Institute for Social Research, 1974). Racial animosities do not flow in only

though racist attitudes are declining (see Table 7, showing changes from 1963 to 1978), many whites are still decidedly racist. For example, in 1978, 49 percent of whites believed that blacks have less ambition than whites, and 25 percent believed that blacks have lower intelligence. Second, the basis for white racism has shifted over time. A generation ago most whites believed that blacks were inherently inferior. Today whites tend to believe that racial differences are cultural: blacks simply have less ambition than whites.[27] Related to this is a third point: whites tend to blame the victims. In 1968, 56 percent of whites said that black disadvantage in jobs, education, and housing were attributable to blacks themselves rather than to racial discrimination.[28] Fourth, white attitudes toward efforts to remedy the problems of blacks vary with the nature of the effort. In 1968, for example, 67 percent of whites favored laws to prevent employment discrimination. But a majority (51 percent) opposed laws to prevent discrimination in the rental or sale of housing.[29] Finally, few whites remain opposed to blacks voting and running for office. But in 1968, 24 percent of whites old enough to vote said they would not vote for a qualified black of their own party preference who was running for office.[30]

In sum, white attitudes toward blacks are now complex, qualified, and ambiguous. Generally, whites no longer regard blacks as inherently and irremediably inferior. But neither do they universally regard blacks as equals.

---

one direction. Surveys reveal that many blacks have negative feelings toward whites. However, it is instructive to notice what pollsters do *not* ask blacks about their attitudes toward whites: They do not ask blacks whether they feel whites are inferior, have lower intelligence, or have lower moral standards.

27. Mildred A. Schwartz, *Trends in White Attitudes* (Chicago: National Opinion Research Center, 1967).

28. Angus Campbell, *White Attitudes Toward Black People* (Ann Arbor, Mich.: Institute for Survey Research, 1971), p. 4.

29. Ibid., p. 23.

30. Ibid., p. 5.

TABLE 7. White Attitudes toward Blacks

Statement	Percentage Agreeing		
	1963	1971	1978
Blacks have less ambition than whites	66	52	49
Blacks are more violent than whites	NA	36	34
Blacks want to live off the handout	41	39	36
Blacks have less native intelligence	39	37	25
Blacks breed crime	35	27	29
Blacks care less for the family than whites	31	26	18
Blacks are inferior to white people	31	22	15

Source: The National Conference of Christians and Jews, "A Study of Attitudes toward Racial and Religious Minorities and toward Women," November 1978, p. 16. Conducted by Louis Harris and Associates.

Political Representation

Political representation is important to categorical groups for three reasons. First, it has symbolic value; it provides the group with a sense of belonging in the society and of participating in that society's public decisions. Second, where there is inequality between groups, those groups will probably have different public policy interests. It is vital that those divergent interests be represented. A related reason is that categorical groups may be in a position to exercise considerable influence over the allocation of certain public goods. Consider the conventional wisdom about the Irish in Boston, who neutralized the political influence of the Brahmins and eventually came to control the allocation of many public goods. With political representation came policies responsive to the needs of immigrants, public sector jobs, and higher social status. The political and social history of the United States is replete with variations on this theme.

It is possible that the representation of blacks by blacks will provide similar benefits. Before we look at the data, these qualifications: First, to suggest that black public officials "represent" black "interests" is to gloss over questions of definition and of behavior. Second, even if black public officials could identify those policies which are in the best interests of blacks, enacting them is another question.[31] However, the data will give us a sense of the presence of blacks among public officials and of how that presence has changed over time.

Blacks are more prominent in politics today than at any time in the past, with the possible exception of Reconstruction. Until the 1960s the only black officials with national prominence were two Congressmen—the flamboyant, mercurial Adam Clayton Powell of Harlem, and William Dawson of Chicago. A third prominent black official was Ralph Bunche, the Nobel Prize winner and member of the United Nations Secretariat. The first black to hold Cabinet rank, Robert Weaver, was not appointed to office until a century after the end of the Civil War. There were very few black officials at the state and local level, save on city councils and school boards.

Table 8 shows how black representation among elected officials has increased in the 1960s and 1970s. The increase can be traced in part to the enfranchisement of Southern blacks by the 1965 Voting Rights Act, to reapportionment, which created more than a dozen congressional districts with black majorities, to the increasing concentration of blacks in cities, and to growing assertiveness by blacks.

Clearly the number of black elected officials has increased dramatically in the past decade. The number of black appointed officials has also increased markedly. But despite these gains, blacks make up less than 1 percent of all elected officials. Even by the most generous criteria we must conclude that blacks are badly underrepresented among public officials.

31. Chapter 3 will discuss voting, which is a primary means for asserting interests.

TABLE 8. Black Elected Officials, by Type of Office

Office and Area	1964	1971	1974	1978
Total	103	1,860	2,990	4,023
Senate				
United States	—	1	1	1
South	—	—	—	—
House of Representatives				
United States	5	13	16	16
South	—	2	4	4
State legislature and executive				
United States	94	198	239	299
South	16	70	89	138
Mayor				
United States	(NA)	81	108	170
South	(NA)	47	63	102
Other				
United States	(NA)	1,567	2,626	4,503
South	(NA)	763	1,454	2,489

Source: Office of Research, Joint Center for Political Studies, Washington, D.C.; and CPR, P-23, No. 54, table 99, p. 151.

A different way to look at these statistics is that in 1978 there was one black Senator for 24 million blacks, as opposed to one white Senator for every two million whites. There is one black Representative for every 1.3 million blacks, as opposed to one white Representative for every 470,000 whites. I am not suggesting here that white officials serve only whites, or that only black officials are responsive to blacks. The point is more subtle: Generally, blacks are far less likely than whites to contact public officials, in part because they *believe* that white officials will not be responsive. This point is elaborated in chapter 3.

Control of Business

Black ownership and control of businesses have several implications for racial equality. First, successful minority-owned business enterprises provide steady and often lucrative income for owners, and the increased social prestige that accompanies economic success. Second, they are a source of pride in the community and provide models for youth. Third, they are a source of investment within minority neighborhoods. Fourth, those who control major economic enterprises are in a position to exercise considerable political influence. If successful black businessmen retain sympathy for the poorer black community, they may be in a position to influence policies affecting large numbers of blacks.

The data on black-owned firms suggest the following. First, most are very small. In 1972, 93.6 percent were sole proprietorships.[32] The average number of paid employees was six.[33] One economist calculates that in 1969 an average profit for small black firms was $7,000, compared to $9,400 for small white-owned firms.[34] Second, the number of black-owned firms has increased over the short run, and total receipts also have increased. In 1969, black-owned firms had receipts totaling $4.5 billion; in 1972, receipts totaled $7.2 billion.[35] Third, the typical black-owned firm is involved in retail sales or personal services (for example, barbershops). Very few firms are involved in manufacturing, wholesale trade, transportation, or extraction industries.[36]

32. U.S., Department of Commerce, Bureau of the Census, *Survey of Minority-Owned Enterprises, 1972: Black* (Washington: Government Printing Office, 1974), p. 6.
33. *CPR*, P-23, no. 54, table 58, p. 84.
34. Timothy Bates, *Black Capitalism: A Quantitative Analysis* (New York: Praeger, 1973), p. 67. Bates's data are based on a survey of enterprises that obtained loans from the Small Business Administration in 1969.
35. Census Bureau, *Minority-Owned Enterprises*, p. 2.
36. Bates, *Black Capitalism*, p. 15.

Fourth, even in those sectors where black enterprise is evident, the market share of black firms is negligible. One estimate is that less than 3 percent of the black food bill is spent in black-owned groceries.[37] It is estimated that black-owned firms receive less than one-half of 1 percent of all receipts for all enterprises combined.[38]

Fifth, black-owned firms have a very high failure rate. This is attributable to several factors: inexperience of black businessmen; undercapitalization due to the difficulties blacks have in obtaining loans; and restricted and volatile markets. Since most black businessmen serve black clientele primarily, their success depends largely on the economic fortunes of the larger black community.[39]

While there are conspicuous exceptions to the general pattern—notably Johnson Publications, Johnson Products, and Motown Industries—black enterprises are generally small, undercapitalized, and local. Although I have no data to support the claim, it is possible that the market share of many black-owned businesses has been affected adversely by racial integration. This would apply to those businesses that had depended heavily on segregated markets—restaurants, hotels, insurance companies, cinemas. Further, few black businessmen exercise political influence outside their own communities. Of those blacks who have achieved national political prominence, very few have been businessmen.[40]

Crime

Blacks have long complained that they were treated unfairly by law enforcement agencies and by the criminal justice system. Blacks were unlikely to be protected by the police, very likely to be assaulted by them, and unable to get fair trials. The data indicate that blacks stand a higher chance of being victims of

37. Robert Kersey, "Vitalize Black Enterprise," *Harvard Business Review* 46 (September/October 1968): 89.
38. Arthur L. Blaustein and Geoffrey Faux, *The Star-Spangled Hustle* (New York: Doubleday, 1972), Appendix.
39. On these points see Bates, *Black Capitalism*, p. 15.
40. The exceptions include Congressmen Diggs and Conyers.

crime than do whites. The victimization rate in 1972 was 132 for blacks, 127 for whites. Blacks are especially likely to be victims of violent crimes; whites are more likely to be victims of theft.[41]

Further, blacks are more likely to be arrested for crimes. In 1972, blacks comprised 42 percent of the jail population nationwide.[42] In part, this may be because blacks are more likely than whites to commit crimes, especially unsubtle, easily detected crimes involving violence or property. But as table 9 indicates, blacks convicted of crimes are likely to be sentenced to longer prison terms than whites. While the raw data do not *prove* that blacks are treated more harshly by the criminal justice system than are whites, the figures are certainly provocative.[43] Blacks are no longer guilty until proven innocent; but it is naive to suppose that racial bias has been purged from the law enforcement and criminal justice systems.

Conclusions

To summarize the clear conclusions: (1) There is unqualified inequality between the races; we have examined no good whose distribution is in favor of blacks. (2) With respect to highly divisible goods such as income and wealth, there exists a situation of strict dominance in favor of whites. (3) Changes over time in the distribution of these goods have generally been am-

41. *CPR* P-23, no. 54, table 106, p. 164.

42. Ibid., p. 170, and table 113, p. 171.

43. It is possible that the discrepancies in sentences are the results of factors other than race, such as prior record, type of plea, and heinousness of crime. For the conventional wisdom that blacks are treated more harshly, see Henry Bullock "Significance of the Racial Factor in the Length of Sentence," *Journal of Criminal Law, Criminology, and Police Science* 52 (1961): 411–17; and Richard Quinney, *The Social Reality of Crime* (Boston: Little, Brown, 1970). For an opposing view, see Carl Pope, "Sentencing of California Felony Offenders," Analytic Report 6, Law Enforcement Assistance Administration, Department of Justice, 1975. Most studies deal with specific jurisdictions, so it is not surprising that their findings vary.

biguous. (4) With respect to those goods whose measurement is more problematic—social status, political representation, law enforcement and criminal justice, and private enterprise—we must conclude that considerable inequality persists.

TABLE 9. Length of Sentence for Persons Sentenced, by Appeal Status, for Selected Types of Crime, 1972

Appeal Status and Type of Crime	Number Sentenced		Median Number of Months Sentenced	
	Black	White	Black	White
Not on appeal				
Murder or kidnapping	1,182	515	66.1	5.8
Rape	126	147	10.7	5.9
Robbery	2,315	834	52.9	11.5
Burglary	2,459	3,370	10.5	10.8
Assault: Aggravated	517	619	13.3	11.1
Simple	649	1,153	6.0	2.6
Larceny: Grand	1,113	755	10.0	10.2
Petty	1,492	1,636	2.9	2.8
Auto theft	625	625	5.6	4.7
Drugs: Sale	1,546	2,388	9.3	5.0
Possession or use	424	951	11.2	5.4
On appeal				
Murder or kidnapping	319	360	548.9	439.7
Rape	123	124	498.9	598.9
Robbery	660	245	236.1	166.8
Burglary	207	510	37.4	86.8

Source: CPR, P-23, no. 54, table 116, p. 174

Justifying Racial Inequality

These inequalities concern representative persons because they have a personal stake in them. Some will be affected favorably by these distributions, others adversely. Since the veil precludes their knowing their fate, they will wish either to find some way to justify the existing inequalities or to eliminate them. Following are some justifications for racial inequality and analyses of their convincingness.

1. Argument from racial differences. One justification begins with the axiom that the races simply *are* unequal. If this is so generally, then specific examples of racial inequality in income, education, and so on, present no problem: they are logically consistent with the axiom. Before we guffaw at this justification, we must recall the survey data presented earlier: a large segment of the white population believes it. However, representative persons who do not know their race are likely to find little merit in a justification that rests on this axiom. And convincing empirical evidence is difficult to come by.

2. Functional criterion of desert. The argument is that some functions are more important and harder to perform than others, and those who perform the most vital and difficult tasks deserve the greatest rewards.[44] As it stands, the argument justifies paying physicians more than postmen. However, it does not justify differences between the races. The principle of desert is irrelevant to the issue of racial inequality.

However, the principle can be made relevant to racial inequality by making another claim—that whites are, by the criterion of desert, more "valuable" than blacks. Our data on occupational status and education suggest that this justification may be acceptable. Whites are on average better educated, and a higher percentage of whites work in the professions and skilled trades.

In order for this justification to be convincing, two further

---

44. For a functional argument for desert, see Kingsley Davis, "A Conceptual Analysis of Stratification," *American Sociological Review* 7 (June 1942): 309–21.

empirical questions must be answered. First, how does it come to be that whites fill the most important positions? Second, if blacks and whites had the same qualifications would they receive the same rewards?

There are two conceivable general answers to the first question. One is that blacks make an unconstrained choice to accept lower paying positions. As a corollary to this choice, they choose also to minimize their human capital investments: they do not attend college because they do not choose to enter occupations that require such training. I know of no data that support this answer. Rather, the evidence points to a second answer—that blacks' choices are highly constrained. Historically, the most important constraint has been racial discrimination. However, major socioeconomic constraints remain, which operate to reduce the educational and career opportunities of blacks.

The answer to the second question is this: If blacks were as deserving by educational and productivity criteria as whites, they would still earn lower incomes. This answer is provided by two different research procedures. One is statistical manipulation that controls for education and productivity.[45] The results of statistical controls are confirmed by more direct research methods. Althauser and Spivack studied more than 800 black and white alumni who graduated between 1931 and 1964 from one predominantly black and two predominantly white universities.[46] Their purpose was to see whether, when blacks and whites are matched with respect to income-producing resources (education beyond the bachelor's degree, job status, years of experience since graduation, and private versus public sector employment), they fared similarly with respect to income.

45. Otis Dudley Duncan, "Inheritance of Poverty or Inheritance of Race?" in On Understanding Poverty, ed. Daniel Moynihan (New York: Basic Books, 1968); Wohlstetter and Coleman, "Race Differences in Income"; and Stanley Masters, Black-White Income Differentials (New York: Academic Press, 1975).

46. Robert Althauser, Sydney Spivack, and Beverly Amsel, The Unequal Elites (New York: Wiley, 1975), pp. 40, 122–23.

While their findings are complex, two results stand out: Blacks generally receive lower salaries, and the disparity increases with years of employment experience.

Whether we consider mean or median income levels, the data show that black graduates almost inevitably receive less income than white graduates. . . . It appears . . . that black graduates actually needed more graduate education in order to obtain comparable jobs, which then paid less than those of their white classmates.[47]

A justification of racial inequality that rests on desert is likely to fall in the face of empirical evidence. Ultimately, whites "deserve" their higher standing largely because they are white.

3. Argument from efficiency. In neoclassical economics, desert is the staff holding up one end of the long banner of inequality. Economic efficiency holds up the other. The argument that inequality is justified on grounds of economic efficiency proceeds as follows: Investment in capital goods is needed for economic growth; savings provide a major source of investment; the wealthy save more than the poor; therefore, economic inequality is necessary for growth. Economic leveling, it is argued, would eventually produce stagnation. Those worst off will benefit more from trickling down of profits from growth than they will from levelling followed by stagnation.[48]

It is clear that this argument is irrelevant to the issue of racial inequality. Even if it were true that inequality among persons is necessary for growth, it does not follow that inequality must

47. Ibid., p. 40. The finding that the black-white income disparity grows with years of work experience implies a warning. In some regions the ratio between young, well-educated blacks and their white cohorts is approaching unity. Althauser and Spivack's results suggest that we should not project the cohorts will remain equal as they grow older.

48. See Martin Bronfenbrenner, *Income Distribution Theory* (Chicago: Aldine-Atherton, 1971); and Paul Davidson, "Inequality and the Double Bluff," *Annals* 409 (September 1973): 25–33.

follow racial lines. Inequality among persons may be inevitable, efficient, or normatively justifiable. Inequality between races is not—unless one wishes to entertain the proposition that racial inequality, per se, is necessary for growth.[49]

4. A final argument is that inequalities in the distribution of goods are statistical artifacts of demographic differences between the races. Two such artifacts are age and region. The black population is younger than the white. Since income increases with age, one would expect the black population to have lower income. Further, close to half the black population lives in the South, where incomes tend to be lower than in other regions. However, previous research has established that these demographic factors are insufficient to account for the inequalities.[50] This explanation is rejected.

Representative persons must conclude that substantive racial inequality persists and that there exists no convincing justification for it. Any reasonable person, acting out of self-interest, must be concerned with a situation that has no justification but may have severe adverse effects on him and his progeny.

Current inequality appears to be the result of past and persisting racial discrimination. But the rules that prescribed discrimination have pretty much been eliminated. Our current rules prescribe that the races be treated equally with respect to

49. One may argue that economic growth in the antebellum South was made possible by slavery. But this is different than arguing that slaves had to be black. For opposing views on the economic efficiency of slavery, see Eugene D. Genovese, *The Political Economy of Slavery* (New York: Vintage, 1965); and Robert W. Fogel and Stanley Engerman, *Time on the Cross: The Economics of American Negro Slavery* (Boston: Little, Brown, 1974). Alexis de Tocqueville may have begun this debate when he observed that the farms of Ohio, where there were no slaves, were more prosperous than the slave-worked farms of Kentucky. See *Democracy in America*, vol. 1, chap. 18, esp. pp. 376–77. Economic efficiency, of course, cannot stand as a moral justification for slavery.

50. See Duncan, "Inheritance of Poverty"; Wohlstetter and Coleman, "Race Difference in Income"; Masters, *Black-White Income Differentials*; and Althauser et al., *Unequal Elites*.

political and civil rights. The question we must confront is: Will new rules, which prescribe procedural equality, also lead to substantive equality? If they will not—if they are closed against racial equality or open so that no inferences can be drawn—then they will be a source of concern to representative persons.

3

Rules of Suffrage and Political Equality

THIS CHAPTER carries a simple but important message: The relationship between rules of suffrage and substantive results is open. From the fact that blacks can vote nothing else follows. The message is simple because it is easy to grasp; indeed, many will find it obvious. And empirical studies serve to convince the doubtful.[1]

The message is important for two reasons. First, despite its obviousness it is often overlooked, causing debates over suffrage to be laced with hyperbole. On the one side, we have been told that voting can lead to creeping mediocrity, majority tyranny, capricious confiscation of wealth, and a host of other evils.[2] Those who support universal suffrage see it as the key to political equality, a vital tool in the protection of the meek, and a way to improve the human condition.[3]

The message is also important because it allows us to place in perspective some long-standing political and constitutional controversies, such as those about white primaries, voting qualifications, and racial gerrymandering. These controversies cannot be appreciated *in vacuo*.They must be seen as attempts to cope with openness by attaching certain conditions that will

1. See for example William Keech, *The Impact of Negro Voting: The Role of the Vote in the Quest for Equality* (Chicago: Rand-McNally, 1968); Donald Matthews and James Prothro, *Negroes and the New Southern Politics* (New York: Harcourt, Brace & World, 1966), especially p. 481.

2. For example, Alexis de Tocqueville, *Democracy in America*, 2 vols., trans. Henry Reeve (New York: Vintage, 1945); Ortega y Gassett, *Revolt of the Masses*(New York: Norton, 1932).

3. Keech offers examples of optimistic predictions about the effect of the 1965 Voting Rights Act. *Impact of Negro Voting*, chap. 1.

affect election outcomes. In this chapter it will become apparent that what lies behind specific arguments is the very definition of political equality. The conclusion will take the form of a question: How does our current view of political equality comport with the reality of a racially divided society?

I will first treat rules of suffrage conceptually, and will identify the necessary conditions under which those rules will produce desirable outcomes for an agent, A. I shall then investigate these conditions empirically, treating them as points of openness affecting the substantive value of voting, focusing on specific controversies and examining how political agencies, mainly the courts, have responded. Finally, I offer some reflections on political equality.

THE GENERAL CONDITIONS

Define rules of suffrage as that set of prescriptions and practices governing voting and elections. Such rules include, but are not limited to, voting qualifications and electoral laws. Rules of suffrage tell us who has the right to vote, how electoral districts are to be drawn, how votes are to be counted, and how winners are to be identified.[4]

Suppose a polity enacts rules of suffrage. Under what conditions can an actor, A, use these rules to secure a public good, x? The general conditions are as follows:

1. The rules must give A the right to vote. Rules of suffrage must contain qualifications for voting, and A may fail to meet those qualifications. Rules of suffrage may limit voting to those of a certain sex, age, race, level of literacy, or wealth. At the time of the ratification of the Constitution, only about a quarter of adult males in the United States were entitled to

---

4. See Douglas Rae, *The Political Consequences of Electoral Laws* (New Haven: Yale University Press, 1971), chap. 2; and Richard Rose, ed., *Electoral Behavior: A Comparative Handbook* (New York: Free Press, 1974) for surveys of suffrage rules. By my definition, the electoral laws Rae describes are a subset of rules of suffrage.

vote.[5] Over time certain qualifications have been eliminated—first wealth, then race, then sex. Some remaining qualifications, including residence, and property ownership in certain bond elections, remain controversial.[6]

2. Actor A must exercise the right to vote granted by the rules. We know that a number of potential voters fail to exercise the right, either because of indifference to election outcomes or because of electoral rules that discourage voting. Compared to other Western democracies the United States has a very low voting turnout, partly because of onerous registration requirements and inconvenient polling times.

3. Actor A must be a member of the winning coalition. Winning coalition is defined variously, ranging from one-person dictatorship to simple majority (super-majority requirements actually mean that a small minority constitutes a winning coalition; unanimity can imply a form of one-person dictatorship).

4. Where decisions are made by representative assembly, condition 3 is much more stringent: Actor A must be a member of a winning coalition of voters, which elects a representative who is a member of a winning coalition of voters in the assembly. Legislative coalitions may be shifting or permanent. Where permanent, they may be parties, regional groups, or races.[7] However, this condition does not require responsible

5. Thomas I. Emerson et al., eds., *Political and Civil Rights in the United States*, vol. 2, 1975 Supplement, p. 1105. This is the best single compilation of major court decisions and commentaries on constitutional issues.

6. On residence, see *Dunn v. Blumstein*, 405 U.S. 330 (1972). Here the Court struck down Tennessee's one-year residence requirement, but did not set a new limit. On property qualifications, see *Salver Land Company v. Tulare Lake Basin Water Storage District*, 410 U.S. 719 (1973). The Supreme Court "upheld a California law providing for the election of the board of a water storage district. Only landowners could vote, and each cast a number of votes proportional to the assessed value of his land." Quotation is from Jonathan Still, "Voter Equality in Electoral Systems" (Ph.D. dissertation, Yale University, 1977), p. 27.

7. Condition 4 assumes a principle of representation under which

parties. With respect to any single policy, x, there will be a winning (and losing) coalition regardless of whether there are parties, responsible or otherwise. But with respect to a range of policies, responsible parties make the shape of winning and losing coalitions more predictable.

5. The desired policy, x, must appear on the agenda. When x is not raised as an issue in the election, A may have no reason to vote. When x is not presented to the representative assembly, it loses by exclusion. There are at least two reasons a policy may not be on a voting agenda. First, it simply may not be regarded as a salient issue. Second, it may fall outside the jurisdiction of voting, at least in the short run. Suppose x were a policy that would condemn drug addicts to death. Such a policy would probably not appear on a legislative agenda because current constitutional rulings would render a vote academic.

Here I have described minimal conditions as simply as possible. If we inject considerations of multiple policy alternatives, shifting coalitions, several representative institutions, and weighted preferences, the conditions become very complex. In practice, they appear less formidable because a number of factors mitigate them. These include logrolling, highly restricted agendas, and means for securing policies that do not involve voting.

These general conditions will next be applied to an analysis of the substantive value of suffrage to blacks. Each condition will be treated as a point of openness. At each point controversies abound, and the way those controversies are resolved affects the precise nature of the relationship between rules of suffrage and policy outcomes. Some controversies, for example the legitimacy of the white primary, have long been settled. But others, such as proportional representation for blacks, are just beginning.

---

voters have interests they express and representatives are expected to reflect the interests of the winning coalition. The real world, of course, is considerably more complex. The classic general text is Hanna Pitkin, *The Concept of Representation* (Berkeley: University of California Press, 1967).

First Point of Openness: The Right to Vote

Let us begin with a rule that states: "The right of citizens of the United States to vote shall not be denied or abridged by the United States or by any State on account of race, color, or previous condition of servitude." This rule, which is the substantive part of the Fifteenth Amendment, was clearly intended to protect blacks from disenfranchisement. But the rule actually confers no obvious benefits. Instead, its substantive value will depend upon the way certain ancillary issues are resolved. Following is a survey of the way the Supreme Court has responded to three of these issues.

1. First, the rule does not grant blacks or anyone else the right to vote. All it says is that where anyone has the right to vote, that right may not be denied to others on grounds of race. The Supreme Court has held that "The States have . . . broad powers to determine the conditions under which the right of suffrage may be exercised. . . . [the] right protected refers to the right to vote as established by the laws and the constitution of the State."[8] A state or subdivision wishing to deny blacks the ballot could simply eliminate certain elective offices, or extend the tenure of incumbents so that blacks' voting rights become academic. Both these devices have been used.[9]

2. Second, the rule states that the right may not be denied by the *United States* or by a *state*. But we know that critical parts of the electoral process are controlled by private agencies— political parties, "better government" leagues, and so on. Obviously, if blacks are excluded from participation in "grass roots" electoral politics, the value of their vote is likely to be neutralized. Two Supreme Court cases, both originating in Texas, expanded the definition of "state action" in electoral politics.

8. *Lassiter* v. *Northampton Election Board*, 360 U.S. 45 (1959).
9. Richard M. Burkey, *Racial Discrimination and Public Policy in the United States* (Lexington, Mass.: Heath Lexington Books, 1971), p. 55.

The first case, *Smith* v. *Allwright*,[10] decided whether the Democratic party of Texas could exclude blacks from membership and thereby from participation in Democratic primary elections. The defendants claimed that the party was a private association and that the state could not control its membership. The Court found that while the party might be a private association, it functioned as an agency of the state. By statute, the state controlled the selection of party officers and other aspects of the primary process. So great was the state's statutory involvement with the party that the Democratic primary constituted state action within the meaning of the Fifteenth Amendment. The Supreme Court held that the amendment could not be "nullified by a State through casting its electoral process in a form which permits a private organization to practice racial discrimination in the election. Constitutional rights would be of little value if they could be thus indirectly denied."[11]

The second case involves even more indirect denial of rights. The Jaybird Association of Fort Bend County was an all-white political group with no formal connection with the Democratic party or with the state of Texas. However, since the association was formed in 1889 it had effectively controlled county politics.

While there is no legal compulsion on successful Jaybird candidates to enter Democratic primaries, they have nearly always done so and with few exceptions since 1889 have run and won without opposition in the Democratic primaries and the general elections that followed.[12]

10. 321 U.S. 649 (1944).
11. *Smith* actually represented the second major attempt by Texas to circumvent the Fifteenth Amendment. In *Nixon* v. *Herndon*, 273 U.S. 536 (1924), the Court reviewed a Texas statute which said, "in no event shall a Negro be eligible to participate in a Democratic Party primary election in the State of Texas." Texas' intent was to have Fifteenth Amendment restricted to the conduct of general elections. The Supreme Court ruled that the statute violated the equal protection clause of the Fourteenth Amendment, but did not address the role of primaries and "private" political agencies in the election process.
12. *Terry* v. *Adams*, 345 U.S. 461 (1953).

The Court found that, given the importance of the Jaybird primary in electoral politics, exclusion from the association was, in effect, a denial of the right to vote on account of race.

The Democratic primary and the general election have become no more than the perfunctory ratifiers of the choice that has already been made in Jaybird elections from which Negroes have been excluded. It is immaterial that the state does not control that part of this elective process which it leaves for the Jaybirds to manage. The Jaybird primary has become an integral part, indeed the only effective part, of the elective process that determines who shall rule and govern the county. The effect of the whole procedures, Jaybird primary plus Democratic primary plus general election, is to do precisely that which the Fifteenth Amendment forbids—strip Negroes of every vestige of influence in selecting the officials who control the local county matters that intimately touch the daily lives of citizens.

Over time, then, the Court has come to construe state action under the Fifteenth Amendment fairly broadly. It is possible that any association involved in electoral politics can be covered by the Court's definition of state action, provided that the association is successful in its influence on elections.[13]

3. The rule we are considering prohibits restricting the right to vote on gounds of race, color, or previous condition of servitude. It follows that surrogates for race are similarly proscribed. Since the grandfather clause was clearly a surrogate for race, the courts had little trouble ruling against it.[14]

The courts were much slower in dealing with voting requirements that, while not objectionable on their faces, were objectionable in use. Such requirements include literacy tests and character references. It has long been common knowledge that

13. In *White* v. *Regester*, 412 U.S. 755 (1973), the Supreme Court considered the role of the Dallas Committee for Responsible Government, a white-dominated group that controlled Democratic party candidate slating in Dallas County, Texas.

14. *Guinn* v. *United States*, 238 U.S. 347 (1915). This case involved congressional elections in Oklahoma.

literacy tests were used to discriminate against blacks. In many parts of the South, whites virtually never failed them and blacks never passed them. But until the 1960s the courts generally failed to consider the discriminatory practices followed under this superficially unobjectionable requirement.[15] Likewise, a requirement that those registering for the first time secure a character reference from someone already registered placed blacks at the mercy of whites.

When the courts began to consider the way superficially neutral requirements were actually used, their opinions could barely refrain from expressing open sarcasm and indignation. The classic case comes from Panola County, Mississippi, which had 7,639 whites and 7,250 blacks of voting age in 1961.

> At least 5,343 white persons were then registered to vote. The only Negro registered to vote in Panola County was R. H. Hightower, 92 years old, who had registered in 1892. This does not tell the whole story, because another Negro, E. G. Holloway, was registered on January 5, 1952, but is now deceased. Also, after this suit was filed and before the trial in the court below, one Houston Potts was registered in April 1962.[16]

The district court was incredulous that the trial court had found no evidence

> that Duke or the state of Mississippi or *anyone else* in Panola County had done anything to intimidate or discourage Negroes from at-

15. In *Lassiter*, the Supreme Court noted that a literacy test might be used to discriminate, but did not examine how it worked in practice. The Court also failed to consider here the continuing effects of past discrimination. North Carolina had replaced its grandfather clause with a literacy test. In counties having permanent registration, whites would not be required to qualify under the new rules, though blacks would be. Thus whites would continue to receive preferential treatment, which originated under the old discriminatory rules. While the Court's decision did not reach this problem, there is some indication the Court would be sympathetic to an appropriately worded appeal.

16. *United States v. Duke*, 332 F.2d 759 (5th Cir. 1969).

tempting to register. The court doubtless intended to say that it found against such evidence rather than that there was "no evidence."

The district court then went on to describe the panoply of abuses that led to a "pattern and practice" of discrimination. Whites were registered immediately, while blacks were forced to wait for hours for an appointment with the registrar of voters. Whites who were demonstrably illiterate had no trouble passing the literacy test, while blacks were given a test that required interpretation of esoteric passages from the Mississippi Constitution:

Some of these are Section 212, dealing with the interest rate on the Chickasaw School Fund, Section 228, dealing with alluvial land, Section 266, dealing with restrictions on state office holding, or Section 282, dealing with the validity of recognizances and other obligations entered into before the adoption of the 1890 Constitution.

Although none of the applicants received word from Mr. Duke as to their success or failure and although the application forms had been destroyed by Duke prior to the trial, he testified that none of them passed. So, also, did some of the witnesses themselves say they either were not satisfied with their answers or they did not complete their answers.

Assuming a few determined blacks could jump these rather high hurdles, they still had to satisfy the character qualifications, which included a procedure by which any qualified elector could challenge the good moral character of an applicant. Once they became sensitive to the way ostensibly neutral rules actually were used, the courts had little trouble identifying pattern and practice.

The courts' new sensitivity to the way rules were used helped blacks overcome discrimination in a number of states. But two major problems remained. First, evidence on pattern and practice required careful observation of process and some reliance on statistical inference. Where the statistics are as overwhelming as those in Panola County, it is relatively easy to infer discriminatory practice, even absent a catalogue of specific abuses. But few cases are so extreme.

Second, even where discrimination was fairly obvious, redress required lengthy and expensive adjudication. A state or subdivision determined to discourage black registration could engage in dilatory tactics for years. The moment one rule or practice was found discriminatory, the state could simply invent a new one. By such devices a state could stay one step ahead of court rulings.

By 1970 the courts and Congress had eliminated a number of requirements that had been used to discriminate. The Twenty-fourth Amendment eliminated poll taxes for federal elections, and in 1966 the Supreme Court extended the proscription to state elections.[17] Literacy tests were abolished by the 1970 amendments to the Voting Rights Act of 1965.[18] These amendments also reduced the closing date for registering for presidential elections to thirty days and eliminated lengthy residence requirements.[19] But it was clearly not possible to eliminate all the rules used to discriminate, especially since many of them, such

17. I do not consider these in detail for two reasons. First, detailed analysis would contribute little to the message of this chapter. Second, some of the Supreme Court's decisions have not rested on the rule currently being considered. For example, decisions on the poll tax were based on the due process clause of the Fourteenth Amendment. See *Harper v. Virginia State Board of Elections*, 383 U.S. 663 (1966); *United States v. Texas*, 252 F. Supp. 234 (W.D. Texas, 1966), aff'd men., 384 U.S. 155 (1966). These decisions, which outlawed the use of the poll tax for state elections, came after ratification of the Twenty-fourth Amendment, which outlawed the use of the poll tax in presidential and congressional elections. A third case, *Herman v. Forssenious*, 380 U.S. 528 (1965), considered that the poll tax had been used to disenfranchise blacks, but the Court's decision rested on the holding that Virginia's election law, which required a federal voter to pay a poll tax *or* file a certificate of residence six months before the election, violated the Twenty-fourth Amendment. Incidentally, when the Twenty-fourth Amendment was presented to Congress in 1962, only five states retained the poll tax as a voting requirement.

18. Title II, Section 201(a).

19. Sections 202(d) and 202(c), respectively.

as prior registration, were not obviously discriminatory and served legitimate purposes.

Congress found a solution to the dilemma by writing a "freezing principle" into the 1965 Voting Rights Act. The act and amendments provide new ways to enforce the Fifteenth Amendment. Its provisions are aimed primarily at the dilatory tactics previously found difficult to address. The relevant provisions include:

1. A list of circumstances that are held to establish prima facie evidence of voting discrimination. The circumstances include use of literacy tests and very low voting turnout—less than 50 percent of voting age population. Originally, the states covered included all or parts of seven southern states—Alabama, Georgia, Louisiana, Mississippi, North Carolina, South Carolina, and Virginia—plus Alaska, Arizona, Hawaii, and Idaho. Amendments to the act in 1970 and 1975 extended coverage so that several other northern states fell under it.

2. Where such evidence exists, the following measures are prescribed:

a. Appointment of federal examiners to supervise the registration of voters and protect against discrimination and intimidation.

b. Prior review and approval of any changes in the covered jurisdiction's voting qualifications or practices. Prior review is intended to guard against the enactment of rules diluting the power of the black vote. In order for new rules to take effect, either the Attorney General or the U.S. District Court for the District of Columbia must issue a declaratory judgment that the rules "will not have the effect of denying or abridging the right to vote on account of race or color."

The requirement for prior review, contained in section 5 of the Voting Rights Act, was intended to prevent jurisdictions from constantly keeping one step ahead of court rulings by introducing a new discriminatory rule the moment an old one was found unconstitutional While the freezing principle of section 5 was found to be an "uncommon exercise of congressional power," the Supreme Court has found it justified by the "exceptional conditions" it was designed to confront.[20]

Further, the Justice Department has held that section 5 places the burden of proof on the state. That is, it is up to the submitting jurisdiction to demonstrate that proposed rules will not have a discriminatory purpose or effect.[21] Because the burden of proof is on the state, section 5 has proved more effective than the Fifteenth Amendment, where the burden of proof is on the plaintiff.[22] However, since the Voting Rights Act applies to only a limited number of states and subdivisions, it is not always useable. Voting discrimination claims seldom rest solely on the Voting Rights Act but generally will also seek support from the Fourteenth and Fifteenth Amendments.

This overview of the Voting Rights Act allows us to understand how cases arise. Covered jurisdictions are required by section 5 to seek prior review of changes in electoral rules. And rules are likely to change frequently. For example, cities frequently change their boundaries through annexation, and annexation is likely to alter the voting power of racial blocs. Further, states are required to reapportion after each decennial census to account for population changes.[23]

In principle, then, wherever whites have the right to vote, blacks also have the right. This means that the right to vote is closed across racial groups. That the rule is closed at this point results from a century of controversy over white primaries and other efforts that served to keep blacks sufficiently uncertain as to their rights that many were discouraged from exercising them. But while the first point of openness has been resolved in principle, government agencies must still work to ensure that

20. *South Carolina v. Katzenbach*, 383 U.S. 301 (1966).

21. David Hunter, *Federal Review of Voting Changes: How to Use Section Five of the Voting Rights Act*, 2d ed. (Washington, D.C: Joint Center for Political Studies, 1975), p. 5; 84 Stat. 314.

22. Emerson et al., *Political and Civil Rights*, p. 32.

23. *Baker v. Carr*, 369 U.S. 186 (1962), established that issues raised by electoral systems are justiciable. The "one man, one vote" ruling is *Reynolds v. Sims*, 377 U.S. 533 (1964).

the right is protected. The need for vigilance is suggested by extensions of the Voting Rights Act that carry its provisions through 1982, and by amendments extending coverage to jurisdictions outside the South.

SECOND POINT OF OPENNESS: EXERCISING THE RIGHT TO VOTE

Having the right to vote does not mean one will vote The United States has long had the lowest voting turnout among Western democracies. Table 10 summarizes some of the differences between the races. The following points require emphasis.

1. Nationwide, black voter participation is lower than white. A smaller percentage of blacks than whites register, and of those who register a smaller percentage of blacks than whites actually show up at the polls. (See table 10.)

2. Generally, voter participation is lower in the South than in the North and West. And blacks in the South participate less than blacks in the North and West. Verba and Nie find that this difference persists when social class is controlled, and attribute it to residual effects of past discrimination.[24] Lower black participation in the South may also be the result of continuing forms of subtle discrimination and intimidation, including placing polling stations in inconvenient locations.[25]

3. For both races, voter participation increases with age, with those in the 45–64 age group registering and voting most frequently.[26]

4. For both races, participation increases with education and socioeconomic status.[27] Verba and Nie argue that low black

24. *Participation in America*, p. 171.
25. See Burkey, *Racial Discrimination*, p. 55. Despite federal efforts, local officials can still make it difficult for blacks to vote. One tactic is to place polling stations in plantation stores where blacks have credit.
26. *CPR*, P-23, no. 54, table 96.
27. Ibid., table 98, shows the positive relationship between years of school completed and voter participation. For a study of the relationship between socioeconomic status and voting, see Sidney Verba and

TABLE 10.   Voter Participation, by Race and Year

	Election Year			
	Congressional		Presidential	
Participation[a]	1970	1974	1968	1972
% VAP[b] registered				
Black	61	55	66	65
White	69	64	75	73
% VAP voted				
Black	44	34	58	52
White	56	46	69	64
% Registered who voted				
Black	72	62	87	80
White	81	73	92	88

Source: CPR, P-23, no. 54, tables 94 and 95.

Note: Since the white population is older than the black, whites have proportionately more members of voting age. This consideration becomes salient when states attempt to apportion districts to create a certain number of black majority districts. See discussion of Beer and United Jewish Organizations, below.

[a] Census Bureau data on voter participation are based on surveys conducted after the fact. Survey respondents tend to exaggerate their participation. While the numbers may be on the high side, the differences between races can be taken at face value, since I have no indication that one race is more prone to exaggeration than the other.

[b] Voting age population.

participation is largely the result of their lower socioeconomic status.[28] It would seem to follow that if black socioeconomic status were to rise relative to white, so would black participation. However, in the short run this point is academic.

_____

Norman Nie, Participation in America: Political Democracy and Social Equality (New York: Harper and Row, 1972), chap. 10.
   28. Participation in America, p. 157.

While black voter participation is lower than white nation-wide, specific environmental variables also affect the level of participation:

5. Civil rights activity and legislation had a tremendous impact on voter participation in the South during the 1960s. Table 11 shows dramatic increases in black registration between 1964 and 1968. One researcher has found that special efforts, especially the presence of federal examiners and the Voter Education Project, had marked effects. In Alabama, Mississippi, and South Carolina, counties with federal examiners and VEP workers had higher registration than those with only an examiner or only VEP workers; and those with one or the other had higher registration than counties with neither.[29]

6. Blacks tend to participate more when race is a salient issue in an election and when the candidates have contrasting positions on race-related issues.[30] This implies that black turnout is high when blacks are seeking office.

7. The above point would lead one to suspect that those blacks who are highly race-conscious participate more than those who are not. The suspicion is supported by Verba and Nie, whose survey revealed that blacks who mention race participate more than blacks who are less race-conscious; indeed, blacks who display group consciousness tend to participate more than the average white.[31]

Aside from the socioeconomic and local environmental factors that affect voter participation, it is likely that turnout is affected by the way elections are conducted in the United States. Barely half of the voting age population actually vote in presidential elections; participation is far lower in off-year and local elections. By contrast, European national elections generally attract more than 90 percent of the electorate.[32] A few compari-

29. Burkey, *Racial Discrimination*, p. 70.
30. I am grateful to Jeanne Fox of the Joint Center for Political Studies for granting me access to the data on which this point is based.
31. *Participation in America*, chap. 10.
32. Information on European elections is obtained from the country studies in Rose, ed., *Electoral Behavior*.

TABLE 11. Voter Registration in Eight Southern
States, by Race

State	Percentage of Voting Age Blacks Registered			Percentage of Voting Age Whites Registered		
	1964	1966	1968	1964	1966	1968
Alabama	23.0	51.2	56.3	70.7	88.1	82.7
Arkansas	54.4	59.7	62.8	71.7	70.3	72.4
Florida	63.7	60.9	62.3	84.0	80.0	83.8
Georgia	44.0	47.2	54.5	74.5	76.7	80.6
Louisiana	32.0	47.1	58.5	80.4	83.1	87.0
Mississippi	6.7	32.9	62.5	70.1	62.9	88.9
South Carolina	38.8	51.4	49.3	78.5	80.2	63.6
Texas	57.7	61.6	83.1	53.2	53.3	72.3

Source: Richard Burkey, *Racial Discrimination and Public Policy in the United States* (Lexington, Mass.: Heath Lexington Books, 1971), p. 54.

Note: These figures, which Burkey obtained from the Voter Education Project, do not jibe precisely with Census Bureau data. For example, Census Bureau data indicate that 71 percent of Southern voting age whites and 62 percent of Southern voting age blacks were registered to vote in 1968. Burkey's figures would seem to produce higher averages for the South. However, the precise figures are not as important as the general trends and cross-racial comparisons. Further, it is not at all unusual for estimates of turnout and registration to vary considerably. See Steven Rosenstone and Raymond Wolfinger, "The Effect of Registration Laws on Voter Turnout," paper presented at the American Political Science Association Convention, Chicago, 1976, table 1 and pp. 5-8.

sons of election procedures in the United States and Europe suggest the reasons.

First, most Western European democracies hold elections on Sundays or holidays. This practice allows voters to avoid the inconveniences associated with trying to fit voting into a workday. Britain, which like the United States holds elections on weekdays, also has comparatively low turnout. And at least one country, Italy, reduces transit fares on voting days to facilitate travel. It is worth noting that of registered voters who did not vote in 1974, 45 percent of blacks and 33 percent of whites said they were unable to go to the polls.[33]

Second, despite the elimination of the poll tax and other impediments, registration in the United States remains more difficult than in most West European polities. In Europe, governments assume responsibility for ensuring that citizens of voting age are registered. In the United States, citizens must assume that responsibility, and the act of registering is often more difficult and time-consuming than the act of voting. Many states require the prospective voter to report in person to a distant county seat, where he must complete long and complicated forms at an office which keeps irregular or inconvenient hours.[34] And some states close registration weeks prior to an election, before campaigns have begun to pique voter interest. Altered procedures, including mail registration and permanent listing, may overcome some of the discouragement in the current system. But such changes would probably not have dramatic effects. A plurality of nonregistered adults (42 percent of blacks, 33 percent of whites) said they did not register because they were "not interested" in politics. Rosenstone and Wolfinger estimate that liberalized registration procedures would increase participation by about 10 percent.[35]

Third, some countries increase turnout by making voting compulsory. Belgium and Australia can impose nominal fines on nonvoters. While the penalties are seldom invoked, such rules do reinforce in people's minds an obligation to vote.[36]

33. CPR, P-23, no. 54, table 97.
34. For a summary of state registration laws, see Steven Rosenstone and Raymond Wolfinger, "The Effect of Registration Laws on Voter Turnout," paper delivered at the American Political Science Association Convention, Chicago, 1976.
35. Ibid.
36. See Keith Hill, "Belgium," and Don Aitkin and Michael Kahan, "Australia," in Rose, ed., Electoral Behavior. One drawback to compulsory voting is an increase in the number of blank or spoiled ballots.

Since our concern is with the low participation of blacks, we must identify those factors that affect the races differently. It appears that while current registration and voting procedures are discouraging, it is not obvious that more liberal practices would advantage blacks disproportionately. Wolfinger and Rosenstone estimate that liberalized registration procedures would have similar effects on the races. In the North, turnout would increase 9.9 percent for blacks, 9.2 percent for whites. In the South, blacks would vote 15.8 percent more, whites 13.5 percent more.

Socioeconomic factors seem to affect the races similarly. But since blacks are worse off, these factors have a disproportionately depressing effect on black turnout. Even if black participation will increase as black socioeconomic status rises, as Verba and Nie project, that fact provides little guidance for the immediate future.

It is also likely that current levels of participation are partly the result of current and past discrimination.[37] These effects can be mitigated by vigilant protection of black voting rights and by grass-roots efforts to increase black interest in politics.

Above all, blacks must see that their votes matter. Unfortunately, black votes often do not matter. Some states have gone to considerable effort to neutralize the impact of black voting. The next section will consider these efforts, and recent responses by the Supreme Court.

THIRD POINT OF OPENNESS: MAKING A VOTE COUNT

The right to vote is a badge of citizenship that is especially important if the right has been long denied. Casting a vote gives

37. Rosenstone and Wolfinger compare black turnout in the North and South, find them similar (when socioeconomic variables are controlled) and conclude that discrimination is absent in the South. An equally plausible inference is that discrimination, or its effects, persists in the North as well as in the South. For example, Northern blacks complain that registration forms from black precincts are processed slowly, and that polling stations in black neighborhoods are provided inadequate numbers of voting machines. See J. Wells, "Voting Rights in 1975: Why Minorities Still Need Federal Protection," *Civil Rights Digest* 7 (Summer 1975): 12–19.

one a sense of participating in an activity that defines a democratic society. But these two things are largely symbolic unless one is a member of the winning coalition. A subset of suffrage rules called electoral laws affects the likelihood that a voter will become a member of a winning coalition. The relationship between electoral laws and black voting is likely to be a source of controversy for some time to come, and this section is intended to shed light on that controversy.

Suppose all blacks and whites had conflicting interests. If this were so, then in elections where those interests were at issue we would expect the races to vote against each other. There are elections in which this occurs—elections in which black and white candidates for office oppose one another. Racial bloc voting is a common phenomenon. Black voters tend to give black candidates an overwhelming proportion of their votes; whites tend to support white candidates.

This is not to say that voters of one race never support candidates of the other race. Obviously, blacks have long supported white candidates. And many black politicians clearly owe their victories to white voters. Los Angeles is only one-quarter black, and Mayor Tom Bradley would not have been elected without massive support from whites. Carl Stokes of Cleveland, Richard Hatcher of Gary, and Kenneth Gibson of Newark needed 10 to 20 percent of white votes to win elections in cities where blacks were not a majority of registered voters.[38] Former Senator Edward Brooke (Republican, Massachusetts) represented a constituency which is only 4 percent black.

Generally, though, it is clear that black politicians are most likely to be successful in districts that are substantially black—where they can win with black votes alone or with overwhelming black support combined with modest white support. With one exception, all black members of the House of Representatives represent districts in which blacks are at least 37 percent of the voting age population. The exception is Ronald V. Dellums, whose Oakland-area constituency is only

38. For a summary of the strategies used by Stokes, Hatcher, and Gibson, see Mark Levy and Michael Kramer, *The Ethnic Factor: How Minorities Decide Elections* (New York: Simon Schuster, 1972).

20 percent black.

So blacks rally to support black candidates, just as white ethnics have long supported members of their groups.[39] We may find racial bloc voting unfortunate, the unhappy residue of an embarrassing and pervasive aspect of American history. But where it occurs certain normative and empirical issues must be addressed.

First, the normative issue: Where it is clear that blacks prefer to be represented by blacks and whites by whites, ought our electoral laws be designed to facilitate those results? Notice that, as a practical matter, one alternative does not exist. Where racial bloc voting occurs, it makes no sense to talk about designing an electoral system that is neutral with respect to race. The choice is between providing institutional representation to both majority and minority categorical groups, or representing only the majority group.

This presents us with a normative dilemma. I believe we would agree that a rule having the effect of completely neutralizing black votes is normatively problematic. But where racial bloc voting occurs the rule of "one man, one vote" may have that effect (except in those few areas where blacks are in a majority). And "one man, one vote" has considerable normative appeal and constitutional support. I shall not attempt to resolve the dilemma here; my purpose is merely to alert the reader to it.

The empirical issue is whether current electoral rules are designed to enhance black representation, or whether they tend to submerge minority votes.[40] Generally, we expect electoral rules

39. On ethnic bloc voting, see ibid.; Harry Bailey and E. Katz, eds., *Ethnic Group Politics* (Columbus, Ohio: Merrill, 1969); Angus Campbell et al., "Membership in Social Groupings," in Bailey and Katz, eds., *Ethnic Group Politics*: J. K. Haddan, L. H. Masotti, and V. Thiessen, "The Making of Negro Mayors," in *Big City Mayors*, ed. L. I. Ruchelman (Bloomington: Indiana University Press, 1969); and Moses Rischlin, *Our Own Kind: Voting by Race, Creed, or National Origin* (Santa Barbara, Calif.: Center for Study of Democratic Institutions, 1960).

40. I am dealing with the narrow but pressing issue of racial bloc voting. The discussion will not treat broader questions of representa-

to produce a positive relationship between number of votes and number of seats. That is, we expect the coalition receiving the greatest number of popular votes to receive the greatest number of legislative seats, just as we expect the candidate who receives the greatest number of votes to "win" the election. Electoral rules that give a minority coalition a majority of seats, or award an election to a minority candidate, would be considered perverse. This is the judgment that produced the Supreme Court's legislative apportionment decision, and it is the specter that motivates attempts to eliminate the Electoral College.[41]

It is also generally the case that electoral systems award more than proportionate shares of legislative seats to coalitions with large shares of the vote, and award less than proportionate shares of seats to coalitions with smaller shares of the vote.[42] This conclusion is derived from a comparative study of electoral systems, and may not be applicable to racial bloc voting in the United States. But if it is applicable, it means we ought not be surprised if a racial minority is "underrepresented" in legislative bodies.

---

tion. Nor do I wish to commit myself to a precise definition of racial bloc voting. There are two issues to be considered in deriving such a definition. The first has to do with the racial "split." When 90 percent of blacks support one candidate and 90 percent of whites support another, we can certainly call this racial bloc voting. But suppose 90 percent of blacks support candidate A and 40 percent of whites also support candidate A. It is not clear we would call this racial bloc voting. The second issue involves the race of the candidates. It is conceivable that 90 percent of blacks will support a white candidate, while whites give overwhelming support to a black candidate. Fortunately for my presentation, this complication has not yet arisen, as far as I know.

41. *Reynolds* v. *Sims.*

42. Rae, *Political Consequences*, p. 70. For Rae, a "large" party is one that receives at least 20 percent of the vote, and a "small" party is one receiving less than 20 percent of the vote. In elections, racial voting blocs are analogous to political parties. Rae succinctly describes the working of electoral systems as the "Sheriff of Nottingham effect": they tend to rob from the weak and give to the strong (p. 86). See also Edward Tufte, "Relationship between Seats and Votes in Two-Party Systems," *American Political Science Review* 67 (June 1973): 540–54.

So we generally expect electoral rules to reward larger over smaller coalitions, and we accept that the rewards (and penalties) are generally disproportionate. What concerns us here is that electoral rules may also be used to exaggerate these general effects of electoral systems.

The electoral rules and devices that affect the relationship between voting and representation are:

1. Electoral formulae. These set minimal criteria for obtaining a seat. There are three general types: majority, plurality, and proportional representation. By definition, a minority bloc loses if a majority of the votes is required to win an election. This formula is therefore least generous to minorities. Plurality formulae award seats to the largest voting bloc; elections conducted under this rule may allow a sizable racial minority to elect a representative whenever the majority race is split among several candidates. Most general elections in the United States are conducted under plurality requirements. Proportional representation is used in only one American electoral system: The lower house of the Illinois State Legislature gives proportional representation to political parties.[43]

2. District size. Minorities are often concentrated geographically. The larger the electoral district, the more likely is a minority to be submerged.

3. District structure. Multimember districts bias outcomes heavily in favor of the majority coalition. At the extreme, a minuscule advantage in the popular vote can give the larger coalition all the seats. Typically, state legislators run in single-member districts, although in 1975 thirty-five states' legislative bodies had at least one multimember district.[44] The vast majority of city councils, on the other hand, are elected from at-large districts. Cities began converting from ward to at-large elections around the turn of the century. The change was motivated partly by a desire to make city governments more efficient, and

43. Malcolm Jewell, "Minority Representation: A Political or Judicial Question," *Kentucky Law Journal* 53 (1965): 267–88.

44. H. Wiltsee, "The State Legislatures," in *Book of the States 1976–77* (Lexington, KY.: Council of State Governments, 1976).

partly by a desire to weaken urban political machines, which depended heavily on ethnic bloc voting. While at-large elections were aimed primarily at white ethnics, at-large district structures now serve to disadvantage racial minorities. In recent years, only one major city, San Francisco, has changed from at-large to ward elections. Blacks in a number of cities, including Houston, Cincinnati, St. Louis, and Richmond, Virginia, have recently brought suit to force a change from at-large to ward structure. Some cities, such as New Orleans, use a combination system: some council seats are filled by ward, others at-large.

4. Ballot structure. In cities using at-large districts to disadvantage minorities, racial and ethnic groups can compensate by using a single-shot voting strategy—concentrating votes on only one or a few of several candidates. However, some cities prevent this strategy by requiring that a vote be cast for every vacant seat. Anti-single-shot rules are clearly intended to disadvantage minority voting blocs.

5. District population composition. One of the most common devices for biasing electoral results is gerrymandering—drawing legislative districts so that some coalitions "waste" votes. The device was first used by Elbridge Gerry to benefit his Massachusetts Federalists, and remains a popular tactic for neutralizing the voting strength of minority parties and racial groups.

6. Special effects. Some polities shape their electoral rules to ensure that certain categorical groups are represented. This is usually achieved through a system of reserved seats, such as those for Harijans (untouchables) in India, Maoris in New Zealand, and blacks in Zimbabwe. As the case of Zimbabwe demonstrates, reserved seats may bear no relationship to the size or voting power of the categoric group. Indeed, occupants of reserved seats may be assigned without voting occurring.

A second special effect, which I shall discuss in detail later, is proportional representation for certain groups. The reader should be alerted to the distinction between *formal proportional representation*, which is an electoral formula used to allocate seats among competing political parties, and *proportional group representation*, which is an effect achieved by manipulating other electoral rules, for example, by gerrymandering districts.

Reserved seats and proportional group representation are closed rules with respect to the number of seats allocated particular groups. Groups may question the number of seats they are allocated, or the way proportions are determined, but the outcome is predictable. Later in this chapter I shall discuss the conditions under which proportional racial representation is likely to occur.

Electoral rules have long been used to minimize and neutralize the potential effects of black voting. Districts have been changed from ward to at-large systems, and single-shot voting has been outlawed.[45] Given the number of ways available to neutralize the effects of black voting, we must ask whether there are restrictions on the use of such rules. For answers I shall turn to recent Supreme Court decisions.

Generally, the courts have regarded electoral rules as nonjusticiable because they involve political questions. The courts' reluctance to become involved stems from the absence of "judicially discoverable and manageable standards" for resolving them.[46] However, in two circumstances the courts have shown willingness to review electoral rules. One involves legislative apportionment cases, where the court has applied the "one man, one vote" standard. The second involves electoral rules that have clear detrimental effects on black voting blocs.[47]

While the courts have found manageable standards for dealing with legislative apportionment, they are still searching for a standard to apply in cases involving racially biased electoral rules. I shall show that, while the Supreme Court's thinking is still in its formative period, it is moving toward the standard of

45. For examples of the way electoral rules can be used to neutralize black voting power, see Lee Sloan, "Good Government and the Politics of Race," *Social Problems* 17 (Fall 1969): 161–74.

46. *Baker v. Carr*, 369 U.S. at 217.

47. Questions about the voting power of racial groups are judicially distinguishable from questions about apportionment. An apportionment plan that satisfies "one man, one vote" could violate judicial standards regarding racial gerrymandering, and vice versa.

proportional representation for racial voting blocs.

The Court first considered racially biased electoral districts in *Gomillion* v. *Lightfoot*, a 1960 case involving racial gerrymandering in Tuskegee, Alabama.[48] In response to the advent of black voting power, the Alabama legislature redrew Tuskegee's city boundaries, transforming it from a square "into a strangely irregular 28-sided figure" which "removed from the city all save only four or five of its 400 Negro voters while not removing a single white voter or resident." The Court found that this action was "not an ordinary redistricting measure even within familiar abuses of gerrymandering," and that the clear purpose of the action, to remove blacks from Tuskegee's voting population, "lifted this controversy out of the so-called 'political' arena and into the conventional sphere of constitutional litigation." The Court then ruled that "when a legislature thus singles out a readily isolated segment of a racial minority for special discriminatory treatment, it violates the Fifteenth Amendment."

Gomillion presented the Court with a singularly unsubtle case. The Court had yet to consider more subtle electoral rules, which diluted black voting strength while allowing blacks to vote. If the Alabama legislature had been less blatant—for example, by removing only a portion of black voters or annexing whites into the city to dilute black voting strength—the Court's task might have been harder.

A broad reading of *Gomillion* would lead to the inference that racial gerrymandering is per se unconstitutional. But Supreme Court rulings should almost never be read broadly. It is clear that what concerned the Court in *Gomillion* was the invidious nature of the action, not the use of racial criteria per se. Further, later legislation, specifically the 1965 Voting Rights Act, is framed in racial terms. The Court has ruled that since the act "necessarily deals with race or color, corrective action under it must do the same."[49]

48. 364 U.S. 339 (1960).
49. *Allen* v. *State Board of Elections*, 393 U.S. 544, 569 (1969).

Still, the search continued for a standard by which to judge dilutions of black voting strength. In *Fortson* v. *Dorsey*[50] and *Burns* v. *Richardson*[51] the Court refused to declare multi-member districts invalid simply because they had the effect of submerging minority voters. What the Court demanded, in addition to proof that the voting strength of racial groups was being canceled or minimized, was evidence that the group was being denied access to the political process:

[I]t is not enough that the racial group allegedly discriminated against has not had legislative seats in proportion to its voting potential. The plaintiff's burden is to produce evidence to support findings that the political processes leading to nomination and election were not equally open to participation by the group in question—that its members had less opportunity than did other residents in the district to participate in the political process and to elect legislators of their choice.[52]

This section of the Court's decision raises two very important questions. First, what type of evidence is sufficient to demonstrate that the political processes "were not equally open to participation to the group in question"? Second, since single-member districts can be gerrymandered to dilute the voting strength of minority groups, will merely substituting single-member for multimember districts satisfy the Court? Let me pose the question differently: The Court says that racial groups have no right to proportional representation *"absent evidence of denial of access to the political process."*[53] Does the Court intend to imply the obverse of this statement; that is, where a racial group shows evidence of denial, does that group then have a right to proportional representation?

An answer to the first question is provided in *White* v. *Regester.*[54] The case involved a district court's ruling that

50. 379 U.S. 433 (1965).
51. 384 U.S. 73 (1966).
52. *Whitcomb* v. *Chavis*, 403 U.S. 124, 149–50 (1971).
53. See Marshall's dissent in *Beer* v. *United States*, 425 U.S. 130, 157 (1975), n. 16. Emphasis added.
54. 412 U.S. 755 (1973).

multimember districts in two Texas counties worked invidiously against minorities. The plaintiffs, blacks in Dallas County and Chicanos in Bexar County, carried to district court the history of minority group exclusion from Texas politics generally and from the political processes of those counties in particular. The white-dominated organization that controlled Democratic party candidate slating in Dallas County did not need black support and used a variety of tactics, including race-baiting, to defeat black candidates. The result was that since Reconstruction only two blacks had been in the Dallas County delegation to the Texas House of Representatives. And the cultural and language barriers suffered by Chicanos "conjoined with the poll tax and the most restrictive voter registration procedures in the nation have operated to effectively deny Mexican-American access to the political process in Texas even longer than the blacks were formally denied access by the white primary."[55] One result was that only five Mexican-Americans had served in the Texas legislature from Bexar County since 1880. Only two of them had come from the barrio where most of the county's Mexican-Americans lived. The Supreme Court found this evidence sufficient to satisfy the burden demanded in *Whitcomb*, and upheld the lower court's invalidation of multimember districts in Bexar and Dallas counties.

Now on to the second question regarding proportional representation. If the Court is suggesting that a form of proportional representation may be appropriate for racial groups, the following additional questions must be raised.

1. Under what conditions will the standard of proportional racial representation (PRR) be applied?

2. When these conditions are satisfied, is PRR to be a standard merely tolerated by the Court, or will it be a standard, *qua* right, which the Court insists upon?

3. Precisely what is meant by proportional representation of a racial group? And who is to decide its operational meaning?

We begin to find answers in two very recent Supreme Court

55. 343 F. Supp. at 731.

decisions dealing with redistricting plans. Officials gerrymandered electoral districts in order to produce rough proportional representation of whites and nonwhites. City council disticts in New Orleans and state legislative districts in Kings County, New York, were drawn so that nonwhites were a majority in a certain number of districts. Assuming racial bloc voting, the result would be proportional representation of racial groups. The Supreme Court has reviewed these cases, and its decisions suggest that it accepts proportional racial representation as a standard for judging compliance with the Fifteenth Amendment and with Section 5 of the Voting Rights Act.

In fact, the standard of proportional racial representation has not been seriously challenged, save by the lone dissent of Chief Justice Burger in the Kings County case. The cases have turned on narrower questions. In the New Orleans case, the parties debated the precise definition of proportionality. And the real issue in the Kings County case was whether a Hasidic Jewish community could be split in order to achieve proportional racial representation. (Later I will distinguish between the Hasidics' real complaint and their constitutional complaint.) These cases deserve extended discussion because they allow us to examine the way the Court looks at the third point of openness, and they suggest answers to the three questions posed earlier.

Since 1954 New Orleans has had a seven-member city council, with one member being elected from each of five districts, and two elected at-large. Blacks comprise 45 percent of the population and 35 percent of the registered voters, but the districts were drawn so that blacks comprised a population majority in none. Voting in New Orleans is by racial bloc, so the result of previous apportionment plans was to exclude blacks from the council.

Following the 1970 census, the five single-member districts were reapportioned so that blacks had population majorities in two districts, but a voting majority (52.6 percent) in only one district. It is at this point that the contestants begin to argue over proportionality. There are two issues here. First, is the unit of analysis to be all seven seats on the city council, or only the five single-member district seats that were reapportioned? Second, if the seats are to be apportioned proportionately by race, which of several possible population proportions ought to be used: proportionate to general population, proportionate to voting age population, proportionate to registered voters? Blacks are 45 percent of the general population, but only 35 percent of registered voters are black; 72.3 percent of the white population is of voting age, but only 57.1 percent of the black population is of voting age.

Although *Beer* raised these questions about proportionality, the Court's ruling did not turn on answers to them. Rather, the majority's decision turned on a principle of nonretrogression: No plan should leave the minority worse off after reapportionment than it was before. Now, since blacks had no representatives on the council, it is difficult to conceive of a plan whose effect would violate the nonretrogression principle. And the new plan, which promised blacks at least one council seat, was clearly an improvement. Justice Marshall's dissent took strong exception to the use of the nonretrogression principle.

While the decision did not turn on a standard of PRR, it is clear that the Court was thinking about it. The Court found that, under the contested plan,

Negroes will constitute a majority of the population in two of the five districts and a clear majority of registered voters in one of them. Thus, there is every reason to predict, upon the District Court's hypothesis of racial bloc voting, at least one and perhaps two Negroes may well be elected to the council under Plan II.[56]

The debate in *Beer* was not over whether proportionality was an acceptable standard, but over which proportion was the correct one. The Court noted this debate (as in the paragraph above), but sidestepped it by introducing the nonretrogression principle and merely noting that rough proportionality is a possible outcome.

56. *Beer* v. *United States*, 425 U.S. at 142.

However, the dissents in *Beer* did confront the issue of proportionality directly. Justice White found that New Orleans' electoral rules and racial bloc voting meant that "no Negro candidate will win in any district in which his race is in a minority." He went on,

In my view, where these facts exist, combined with a segregated residential pattern, Section 5 (of the Voting Rights Act) is not satisfied unless, to the extent practicable, the new electoral districts offered the Negro minority the opportunity to achieve legislative representation roughly proportional to the Negro population in the community.[57]

Justice Marshall's strong dissent (joined by Justice Brennan) chides the majority for sidestepping the central issue: "Essentially we must answer one question: when does a redistricting plan have the effect of 'abridging' the right to vote on account of race or color?"[58] For Marshall, the majority's answer—nonretrogression—is hardly sufficient; the most acceptable standard is that of proportional racial representation.[59] However, he does not advocate PRR without qualifications. He supports the *Whitcomb* dictum that "there is no right to proportional representation absent evidence of denial of access to the political process." Marshall finds ample evidence that blacks in New Orleans were denied access.

Marshall's dissent also takes issue with the Court's blindness to the two at-large districts. He concedes that the case, as presented, allows review of only the five single-member districts. However, he argues that the Court must consider the fact that there are seven seats to be filled.

Proportional representation of Negroes among the five district seats on the council does not assure Negroes proportional representation on the entire council when, as the District Court found, the two at-large

57. Ibid. at 143–44.
58. Ibid. at 145.
59. Ibid. at 156–57.

districts will be occupied by white-elected members. The Court's approach of focusing only on the five districts would allow covered municipalities to conceal discriminatory changes by making them a step at a time, and sending one-, two- or three-district alterations to the Attorney General for approval. If nothing beyond the districts actually before him could be considered, discriminatory effects could be camouflaged and the prophylactic purposes of the act readily evaded. . . . Under the Court's approach, the smaller the number of seats that the city may present for consideration, the grosser the discrimination that may be tolerated.[60]

While it is clear that the Court and the contestants are talking about proportional racial representation, the Court chose to settle on the milder standard of nonretrogression. This allowed the majority to avoid answering some of the hard questions attached to PRR.

The Court was afforded another opportunity to consider proportional racial representation in *United Jewish Organizations v. Carey*.[61] The case arose out of a redistricting plan in Kings County, New York. Three facts about the case concern us here. First, the plan set out explicitly to achieve proportional representation of whites and nonwhites in the Kings County delegation to the state legislature. It did this by establishing nonwhite majorities in approximately 30 percent of the county's senate and assembly districts. (The county is approximately 35 percent nonwhite.) Given racial bloc voting this would mean that nonwhites would send delegates (presumably nonwhites) from 30 percent of the districts.[62]

Second, the plan set quotas for within-district majorities. Variation in the size of nonwhite majorities was controlled, so

60. Ibid. at 159 and n. 19.
61. *United Jewish Organizations of Williamsburgh v. Hugh Carey*, 45 L.W. 4221 (1977).
62. As it happened, most of the nonwhite majority districts returned whites to the state legislature. But the districts were constructed so that nonwhites would have been elected had they run and had nonwhites turned out to support them.

that seven assembly districts had nonwhite majorities of at least 65 percent and no more than 90 percent. The three nonwhite majority senate districts were made 70 to 75 percent nonwhite. The supermajority quotas were intended to compensate for lower nonwhite registration rates, a phenomenon caused in part by the fact that the nonwhite population is younger.[63] Third, in order to achieve these quotas, the plan required that the Hasidic community, which under a 1972 plan had been placed in one assembly district and one senate district, be divided between two senate and two assembly districts.

The petitioners, suing on behalf of the Hasidic community, had three constitutional objections. First, they charged that the use of racial criteria in districting and reapportionment is never permissible. Second, petitioners claimed that dividing the Hasidic community "would dilute the value of each plaintiff's franchise by halving its effectiveness."[64] Third, they charged that New York's specific use of the 65 percent quota was unconstitutional.

The Court had little trouble dismissing the first complaint. Racial classifications are not forbidden, and the Court has

63. See *United Jewish Organizations* v. *Carey* 45 L.W. at 4226, n. 22; and intervenor brief submitted by the NAACP Legal Defense Fund, esp. p. 46 and Appendix, p. 219. Lower nonwhite registration rates may also be caused by other factors. See generally Verba and Nie, *Participation in America*; Donald Matthews and James Prothro, "Social and Economic Factors and Negro Voter Registration in the South," *American Political Science Review* 57 (March 1963): 24–44; Matthews and Prothro, *Negroes and the New Southern Politics*.

64. *United Jewish Organizations* v. *Carey*, 45 L.W. at 4223. A bit of reflection reveals the first two complaints to be mutually contradictory. In essence, the Hasidics are claiming simultaneously that (1) the Constitution prohibits establishing new districts on the basis of race, and (2) the Constitution protects their group from being split. Now if racial or ethnic considerations cannot be used to establish new districts, it follows that they cannot be used to demand retention of old districts. Absent the constraints of constitutional gamesmanship, I suspect the Hasidics would have dropped their first complaint and claimed merely that their group wanted the same consideration afforded blacks.

ruled that in some circumstances racial criteria are necessary. With respect to voting, the Court ruled in 1969 that since the 1965 Voting Rights Act "necessarily deals with race or color, corrective action under it must do the same."[65] Since the contested plan was an attempt to comply with the act, the plaintiffs had no sound objection.

The Court also had little trouble disposing of the plaintiffs' claim that their vote was being diluted. Before the Supreme Court the plaintiffs made this disposition easy by presenting themselves as white voters rather than as Hasidics. The Court held the following: Whites comprised 65 percent of the county population, but "the plan left white majorities in approximately 70% of the assembly and senate districts in Kings County."[66] As a group, then, the whites in Kings County received "fair representation."

In individual districts where non-white majorities were increased to approximately 65%, it became more likely, given racial bloc voting, that black candidates would be elected instead of their white opponents, and it became less likely that white voters would be represented by a member of their race; but as long as whites in Kings County, as a group, were provided with fair representation, we cannot conclude that there was a cognizable discrimination against whites or an abridgement of their right to vote on grounds of race. Furthermore, the individual voter in the district with a non-white majority has no constitutional complaint merely because his candidate has lost out at the polls and his district is represented by a person for whom he did not vote. Some candidate, along with his supporters, always loses.[67]

This small section of the Court's decision speaks volumes, and also glosses over a fair number of issues. I shall emphasize three points. First, the Court recognizes conditions under which it makes sense to consider whether a racial group receives rep-

65. *Allen v. State Board*, 393 U.S. at 569.
66. *United Jewish Organizations v. Carey*, 45 L.W. at 4227.
67. Ibid.

resentation. Second, it is groping for some definition of "fair representation" of racial groups. That standard appears to be rough proportionality. Third, the Court received the appeal in a way that allowed it to avoid the touchy question of whether Hasidics as a group (as opposed to whites as a group) had standing to sue under the Fourteenth and Fifteenth Amendments and the Voting Rights Act. Now assuming Hasidics vote as a bloc, it is quite likely that the contested plan, which divided the community between districts, would dilute the effectiveness of the Hasidic vote. But the complaint was not phrased in these terms before the Supreme Court, possibly because the district court and court of appeals had ruled that the "petitioners enjoyed no constitutional right in reapportionment to separate community recognition as Hasidic Jews."[68] Petitioners chose not to challenge this holding, and thereby allowed the Supreme Court to avoid deciding whether this group, in addition to Puerto Ricans in New York, Mexican-Americans in Texas, and blacks, are entitled to separate community recognition.

With respect to the specific within-district quotas established under the New York plan, the Court seemed to reason as follows: (1) The purpose of black majority districts is to increase the likelihood that black voters will be able to elect whichever representative they wish. (2) Such a purpose is constitutionally permissible, following *Beer*. (3) It follows that a state may establish within-district majorities of a size necessary to reach that purpose.

This rough syllogism had to be reconstructed from the decision, because the Court actually confuses two types of "quotas." One type involves how many majority districts there must be. The other involves the size of black majorities within a district.[69] In spite of the confusion the Court appears to be saying this: First, it will review questions about the number of black-majority districts established. Such a review will apply the nonretrogression principle as a minimal standard[70] and will al-

---

68. Ibid. at 4224.
69. This point is suggested in ibid., at 4226, para. 2.
70. Ibid at 4225.

low proportional racial representation: "the Constitution permits [a state] to draw district lines deliberately in such a way that the percentage of districts with a non-white majority roughly approximates the percentage of non-whites in the county."[71]

Only one member of the Court, Chief Justice Burger, is unwilling to approve such an outcome.[72] And three members of the Court, White, Brennan, and Marshall, appear willing to require that districts be drawn to produce rough proportional racial representation when the following conditions apply: (1) where there is racial bloc voting; (2) where electoral rules, such as anti-single-shot laws, disadvantage minorities; (3) following *Whitcomb*, when evidence exists that racial minorities have been denied opportunity to participate in the electoral process; and (4) when residential segregation exists. (The last condition merely recognizes that racial gerrymandering would be tortuous in integrated neighborhoods.)[73] It is unlikely that a majority of the Court is willing to require proportional racial representation. However, the New York case makes clear that a majority will tolerate such special effects when they are taken to comply with the Voting Rights Act.

Second, the Court will review questions regarding the size of nonwhite majorities within districts. However, the Court has not developed a standard, equivalent to the nonretrogression principle, to apply here, and it is therefore likely to defer to the judgment of the state.

The State must decide how substantial those majorities must be in order to satisfy the Voting Rights Act. The figure used in drawing the *Beer* plan, for example, was 54% of registered voters. At a minimum and by definition, a black majority district must be more than 50% black. But whatever the specific percentage, the State will inevitably arrive at it as a necessary means to ensure the opportunity for the elec-

71. Ibid. at 4227.
72. Ibid. at 4231.
73. These conditions are explicated by Justice White in his dissent from *Beer* v. *United States*, 425 U.S. at 143.

tion of a black representative and to obtain approval of its reapportionment plan.[74]

We think it was reasonable for the Attorney General to conclude in [Kings County] that a *substantial* non-white majority—in the vicinity of 65%—would be required to achieve a non-white majority of eligible voters.[75]

Our conclusions are as follows:

1. The relationship between even complete minority voting and even minimal minority representation is open.

2. Electoral rules can influence whether minority voting will lead to minority representation.

3. Where there is racial bloc voting, the issue of minority representation becomes highly salient.

4. At least since *Gomillion* in 1960, the Court has shown concern that electoral rules not neutralize the voting power of minorities.

5. The Court will use the principle of nonretrogression to ensure that minority voting power is not reduced.

6. The Court will allow states to establish electoral rules that allow rough proportional representation of racial groups. Such rules would make the relationship between voting and representation closed. But the conditions under which the Court will allow such electoral rules are rather narrow.

7. It is unlikely that the present Court will *require* that districts be drawn to enhance the likelihood of proportional racial representation.

8. The range of options between nonretrogression and proportional racial representation is very broad. The Court will protect minorities from a worsening of their voting power, but only the states can enhance voting power, absent more stringent requirements by the Court.

74. *United Jewish Organizations* v. *Carey*, 45 L.W. at 4226. Actually, the Beer plan produced black population majorities in two districts and a black voter majority of 52.6 percent in one district. See 425 U.S. at 136.

75. *United Jewish Organizations* v. *Carey*, 45 L.W. at 4527. Emphasis in text.

9. The Court has not defined some of the terms it used in the *Beer* and Kings County cases. For example, it is not clear what racial bloc voting means. And, as Marshall notes in his *Beer* dissent, it is not always clear when an electoral rule enhances or reduces voting power. The Court will probably avoid establishing rigid definitions and rely instead on case-by-case evaluations.

10. The Court has not yet addressed the unit-of-analysis problem raised by Marshall's *Beer* dissent. In *Beer* the Court felt the two at-large seats irrelevant to its discussion of proportionality, but offered no justification for this position save that the state redrew only the five single-member districts. The unit of analysis was not contested in *United Jewish Organizations*, so the Court did not confront it, save to suggest that proportional representation in the aggregate is sufficient to compensate for lack of representation in a particular district.

FOURTH POINT OF OPENNESS: PRODUCING WINNING COALITIONS

Proportional racial representation would probably increase the benefits of black voting. Under such a rule, whenever blacks are a substantial portion of the electorate, they would be virtually assured of some voice in legislative chambers—assuming racial bloc voting of course.

The mere presence of blacks would provide symbolic benefits. It might also inject a new sensitivity into legislative bodies—a sensitivity to the problems of blacks and other disadvantaged minorities. The agendas of legislative bodies would be shifted a bit, both with regard to the types of issues raised and to the way those issues are discussed. Further, black legislators give black citizens a contact point. This would overcome one of the major impediments to black political participation—the reluctance to contact legislators about problems.[76]

76. Verba and Nie, *Participation in America*, chap. 10, find that a major difference in participation between blacks and whites is in

More black lawmakers would mean an altered agenda—not a dramatic change, but a slight shift in emphasis and sensitivity. Such a shift might reduce the frequency of dramatic demonstrations, which blacks have often felt were necessary to draw attention to their problems. Lacking permanent representation in policymaking institutions, blacks took to the streets in the 1960s, sometimes in well-planned demonstrations, occasionally in spontaneous and violent outbursts. For example, Sears and McConahay argue that the Los Angeles riot of August 1965 was, in part, the "functional equivalent" of an institutionalized voice:

The politics of violence was aimed not so much at personal reform, then, as at inducing powerful whites at all levels and in all areas of society to redress blacks' grievances and to open up fairer and more routine procedures for grievance redress.[77]

Blacks felt they were unable to influence public policy through conventional electoral politics so they had little choice but to use unconventional tactics.[78]

But there is a certain irony to this explanation of the Watts riot. Superficial evidence suggests that Los Angeles blacks were actually better represented than blacks in most urban areas. At the time of the riots there were three black city councilmen (including Thomas Bradley), two black state assemblymen (including Mervyn Dymally), and one black congressman (Augustus Hawkins).

One explanation for the apparent irony is this: Even if those black elected officials were able to represent black grievances, and even if they altered legislative agendas to incorporate them,

---

citizen-initiated contacts. Blacks are far less likely to contact public officials, especially local officials. The reluctance is pronounced in the South.

77. David Sears and John McConahay, *The Politics of Violence: New Urban Blacks and the Watts Riot* (Boston: Houghton Mifflin, 1973), p. 105.

78. Ibid., pp. 62–63.

their votes alone were insufficient to protect or promote black interests. Here is the final rub. Even proportional racial representation, which would maximize black voting strength, will not of itself produce policies favorable to blacks. Where black and white interests conflict diametrically, blacks will lose, save in those few local areas where blacks are in the majority. The winning (majority) legislative coalition will favor whites.

There are few instances in which black and white legislators take diametrically opposed positions. But such racially distinct coalitions are certainly possible and they occur occasionally. We know, for example, that on a wide range of public policy issues, modal black opinion is different from modal white opinion. The differences are especially pronounced with respect to welfare policies and civil rights. For example, in 1974, 74 percent of blacks favored federal open housing legislation; a majority of whites opposed it.[79] Certainly one would expect the races to disagree over affirmative action. On a different front, one suspects that United Nations Ambassador Young's statements—that the South African regime is illegitimate, that a number of American officials are racists—would elicit agreement from blacks despite the howls of protest they provoked among white journalists and officials.

One hopes that racially divisive policy issues can be avoided. But where they arise, the outcome is predictable: Blacks will lose.

A SEARCH FOR POLITICAL EQUALITY

Nothing I have said should be taken to mean that I think voting has no value for blacks or that it has only symbolic

---

79. See Sandra Kenyon Schwartz and David Schwartz, "Convergence and Divergence in Political Orientations between Blacks, and Whites," *Journal of Social Issues* 32, no. 2 (1976): 153–68; Norval Glenn, "Recent Trends in White-Nonwhite Attitudinal Differences," *Public Opinion Quarterly* 38 (Winter 1974–75): 596–604. Glenn finds increasing dissensus, even on issues not directly race-related, e.g., the death penalty.

value. It is clear that black votes, and changes in electoral rules enhancing the effectiveness of black votes, have increased dramatically the number of blacks elected officials. That in itself is a worthwhile gain. Further, black voting power has probably brought about a number of changes in the behavior of white elected officials. We frequently hear how former staunch segregationists have changed their behavior in order to woo black voters. And there is probably spillover into the behavior of appointed officials.

What I am suggesting is that there is nothing in rules of suffrage that would lead us to predict that black voting will have an effect on policy. If black voting is to have predictable effects on policy certain conditions must be satisfied; and they have not been.

However, there are two general situations that will allow blacks to achieve desired policy ends in the face of open rules of suffrage. The first is a situation that allows blacks to engage in logrolling, taking advantage of political divisions and forming the pivotal point of a winning coalition. The second is one in which generous white majorities do what blacks ask because they think they should do so.

Minority coalitions are most effective when their votes are unpredictable. Otherwise they have little bargaining power. Unfortunately for the logrolling strategy, black voting patterns in general elections and in legislatures are fairly predictable. The second situation lacks the power component implied by political equality. A group that relies on generosity will be indifferent to its source. A benevolent king is as acceptable as a democratic legislature, a despot no worse than a hostile majority.

It should now be clear that what is at issue here is the very meaning of political equality. We do not have a concept of political equality appropriate to a racially divided society. The liberal conception, which emphasizes rights of individuals and "one man, one vote," is clearly not equipped to handle conflicts between permanent identifiable groups. John Stuart Mill recognized that problem more than a century ago. Mill, like de Tocqueville before him, feared that the interests of a minority would be trampled by the votes of the majority. For both Mill and de Tocqueville the minority in question was the elite, which would always be outvoted by an unsophisticated *demos*. Mill's solution was a form of proportional representation that could guarantee the aristocracy a voice in legislatures.[80]

The problem Mill never addressed was that legislative voice does not mean winning legislative coalitions. Proportional representation would guarantee minority representation, but would not necessarily protect minority interests. Further, it has never been clear what "one man, one vote" means; nor is it clear why majorities should rule—even in a society that approximates the preconditions of liberalism. In spite of its long use there does not exist a convincing philosophical justification for majority rule.[81]

The pluralist view of political equality does incorporate groups. Pluralism assumes that there is no such thing as a permanent majority or a permanent minority. Rather, majorities are ephemeral, formed by shifting coalitions of interest groups.

80. See "Considerations on Representative Government," in *On Liberty, Representative Government, the Subjection of Women* (London: Oxford University Press, 1966), chap. 7. Another solution, practiced in Britain and Belgium, was plural voting. Persons were allotted additional votes if they held university degrees or owned a certain amount of property. De Tocqueville thought that certain institutions, notably the courts and the legal profession, would exercise a conservative influence sufficient to mitigate majority tyranny. See *Democracy in America*, vol. 1, chap. 16.

81. On the Supreme Court's confusing conception of "one man, one vote," see Still, "Voter Equality." John Locke, the father of liberalism, justified majority rule simply: "it is necessary the body should move that way whither the greater force carries it, which is the consent of the majority." This is hardly convincing. See "An Essay Concerning the True Original, Extent and End of Civil Government," in *Social Contract*, ed. Sir Ernest Barker (London: Oxford University Press, 1975), para. 95. Robert Paul Wolff claims to have invested considerable energy in his futile search for a convincing justification for majority rule. See *In Defense of Anarchism* (New York: Harper Torchbooks, 1976). Wolff places much stronger normative demands on a decision rule than I do.

Pluralism, then, envisions rule by minorities: no group loses consistently, and no group is likely always to be in the winning coalition.[82] The coalition that supports higher tariffs is different from the coalition that supports farm subsidies, which is different from the one supporting national health insurance. As a description of the way coalitions of regional or economic groups form to support their interests, pluralism may be acceptable. But it appears inadequate to handle conflicts between majority and minority races.

It is obvious that the majority will occasionally support policy favorable to the minority. The Civil War Amendments of the past century and the civil rights legislation of the past decade provide examples. But we cannot mention these examples without remembering the decades of delay and conflict that preceded them. Clearly these were decades, indeed centuries, when legislation strongly favored by blacks was opposed adamantly by whites. The pluralist view of political equality affords little comfort to blacks subjected to this racist form of majority tyranny.[83]

The Marxist view of political equality is premised upon the elimination of social classes. Marxist analysis is therefore inadequate on several grounds. First, it is not clear that racial inequality and class inequality are analogous, or that one can treat racial inequality as a special case of class inequality.[84] Where

82. The pluralist conception originally appeared in Federalist Paper 10, written by James Madison. It is elaborated by Robert Dahl in *Preface to Democratic Theory* (Chicago: University of Chicago Press, 1956).

83. See J. L. Stanley, "Majority Tyranny in Tocqueville's America: The Failure of Negro Suffrage in 1846," *Political Science Quarterly* 84 (Spring 1969): 412–35; and L. L. Smith, "Harry Smith, Negro Suffrage, and the Ohio Constitutional Convention: Black Frustration in the Progressive Era," *Phylon* 35 (June 1974): 165–80.

84. Although we frequently hear racial issues discussed in Marxist class terms, very few scholars have tried to work out this type of analysis. See Paul Baran and Paul Sweezey, *Monopoly Capital: An Essay on the American Economic and Social Order* (New York: Monthly Review Press, 1966), chap. 9; and Robert Blauner, *Racial Oppression in America* (New York: Harper & Row, 1972). The best attempt is by

the economic relationship between the races is one of perfect dominance, class analysis may be appropriate. But chapter 2 demonstrates that the relationship between the races in the United States is one of strict dominance: generally whites are better off than blacks, but there are many well-off blacks and many poor whites. Latter-day Marxists have attempted to account for this situation by introducing the term "underclass" to describe a race that is on average worse off than another race. While the term allows more realistic descriptions, it sacrifices the elegance of standard Marxist class analysis.[85]

Second, as an empirical matter, we know that no society has achieved complete economic leveling. It is possible that partial economic leveling, were it attempted in the United States, would still leave blacks at the bottom of a truncated socio-ecomonic hierarchy. Partial leveling does not mean that the relative positions of blacks and whites would change.

Third, we know that economic leveling requires considerable

William J. Wilson, *The Declining Significance of Race: Blacks and Changing American Institutions* (Chicago: University of Chicago Press, 1978)

Since blacks' life chances are no longer determined strictly by race, Wilson argues that class is now at least as important as race. Most blacks just happen to be members of the underclass. In a legal sense, Wilson's first premise is correct: race, per se, is not allowed to determine life chances. However, from this it does not follow that class is the obvious alternative form of analysis. Nor is Wilson convincing. For example, he claims that "the center of racial conflict has shifted from the industrial sector to the sociopolitical sector" (p. 150). By this and similar statements he appears to undermine the usefulness of class analysis.

Further, there is some confusion about the type of class analysis Wilson wishes to use. By stating that poor whites are part of the underclass (p. 154), he seems to diverge from formulations used by John Leggett and Anthony Giddens, and moves toward the conventional meanings of *Lumpenproletariat* in traditional Marxist writing. See John Leggett, *Class, Race, and Labor* (New York: Oxford University Press, 1968) p. 14; and Anthony Giddens, *The Class Structure of The Advanced Societies* (New York: Harper & Row, 1975), p. 112.

    85. Giddens, *Class Structure*, p. 112.

political authority. Where economic inequality is reduced, other forms of inequality may increase. It will do us little good to trade economic inequality for political inequality if our original concern is with political inequality.

What we must search for is a concept of political equality that considers the following harsh fact: Whenever the interests of the black minority conflict with the interests of the white majority, blacks will lose. The concept adequate to this situation may also be adequate to its obverse—that is, a society such as Zimbabwe-Rhodesia or South Africa where black majority rule is imminent. Incidentally, the reader who has thus far lacked sympathy for my complaints about black under-representation should ask himself the following question: "If I were a white Rhodesian, would I consider proportional racial representation adequate to protect my interests?"

But the reader may think this analogy unfair. Despite its vicious racist history the United States is, at present, a far cry from Rhodesia and South Africa with respect to racial inequality. Recent legislation was intended to ensure equal treatment and equal opportunity, to purge the nation of racial discrimination and allow blacks to enter the mainstream of American life. While the races may have modally different interests today, those differences need not be permanent. If blacks continue to advance economically, so that they achieve rough equality with whites, a major source of racial conflict will dissipate. As the races come closer together in socioeconomic status, their demands on a wide range of public policy issues will also come together. And where interests are similar, representation becomes less salient. If blacks and whites agreed on public policy it would not matter much whether blacks voted or had black representatives.

In the next chapter I will examine whether socioeconomic equality between the races is likely to happen. I do this by examining a rule by which economic goods are distributed. That rule is equal opportunity.

4

Equal Opportunity and Economic Equality

MY PRIMARY TASK in this chapter is to examine the relationship between equal opportunity and equal result. I shall ask whether a rule of equal opportunity can be expected to produce rough substantive equality between the races. As in previous chapters, I shall continue the theme of open and closed rules. However, it is not possible to state at the outset whether equal opportunity is an open or closed rule with respect to the distribution of goods. That will be revealed as the chapter progresses.

The discussion of equal opportunity provides a backdrop against which to examine three other major issues. One is the perplexing disparity between black and white unemployment rates. I shall show that the disparity is actually one of the perverse results of the rule of equal opportunity. Next I shall take up the issue of affirmative action in employment, and show that it intends merely to achieve the results we can legitimately expect from equal opportunity. The third issue I shall address is the "white ethnics ploy"—the flawed but apparently appealing argument that blacks can be expected to replicate the experiences of white immigrant groups.

THE LIBERAL VIEW OF EQUALITY

Our investigation of the relationship between equal treatment and equal result must begin with the understanding that the United States has always held a special and limited view of equality. Ours aspires to be a liberal society, and we understand equality in its liberal sense.[1] Indeed, our traditional view

1. See Louis Hartz, *The Liberal Tradition in America* (New York:

of equality is even more restricted; it is distinctly Lockean.

In John Locke's liberalism, equality stands alongside two other principles, liberty and property. These principles, derived from a hypothetical state of nature, seemed to Locke to be mutually supportive. The protection of property was the major reason for abandoning the state of nature to enter civil society.[2] The important thing was that there be equality of rights with regard to property. A commander had a right to send a soldier to almost certain death, but he could not appropriate one penny of the soldier's money.[3]

From the idea that men had equal freedom in the state of nature Locke derived rules for limitations on civil government, and the need for majority rule. Since every individual is to count as one (otherwise, there is not equality), "it is necessary the body should move whither the greater force carries it, which is the consent of the majority."[4]

Although Locke argued for equal property rights, he accepted that there would be inequality in the distribution of property, stemming mainly from unequal wills and abilities. There had once been enough land for everyone. But no man would claim more than he needed to fill his immediate needs. There was no surplus in the state of nature, hence only small inequality, and that the just result of unequal effort. The development of money made surplus possible, and increased inequality. "And as different degrees of industry were apt to give men possessions in different proportions, so this invention of money gave them the opportunity to enlarge them."[5] The advent of

---

Harcourt, Brace, and World, 1955); and Sanford Lakoff, *Equality in Political Philosophy* (Boston: Beacon Press, 1964). Lakoff traces the development of three concepts or traditions of equality: liberal, socialist, and conservative.

2. "An Essay Concerning the True Origins, Extent and End of Civil Government," in *Social Contract: Essays by Locke, Hume and Rousseau*, ed. Sir Ernest Barker (London: Oxford University Press, 1975), pp. 1–143.

3. Ibid., chap. 11, para. 139.

4. Ibid., chap. 8, para. 95.

5. Ibid., chap. 5, para. 48.

money affected inequality quantitatively but not qualitatively.

Locke wrote before the Enclosure Movement in England, before the Industrial Revolution, before the classical economists had revealed the importance of scarcity, before industrial capitalism alienated man from the fruits of his labor. His view of equality "presupposed a simple agrarian economy where labor was virtually the sole factor of production."[6] By the beginning of the nineteenth century, pastoral liberalism had been undermined by social change. It was left to John Stuart Mill and other nineteenth-century liberals to bring Locke's doctrines up to date.

Ironically, at the very time the Industrial Revolution in England was sounding the death knell of Locke's pastoral liberalism, developments in the United States were giving it new life. While the younger Mill struggled to adapt Locke's principles to the ugly realities of Manchester and Liverpool, Horatio Alger and Horace Greeley were converting them into the mythic stuff of the American success ethic—hard work, luck and pluck, going west to grow up with the country. However much the rags-to-riches rhetoric of nineteenth-century America may have diverged from social reality, it was the rhetoric that formed the core of belief. "In the beginning," Locke wrote, "the whole world was America."[7] In the end, America was to be the proving ground for liberalism and for the liberal view of equality.

In the United States, liberalism did not confront the social conflicts and philosophical alternatives that gave it such trouble in Europe. A liberal tradition was brought to the United States by the same striving middle class that had embraced it enthusiastically in England. The new land lacked a titled aristocracy sympathetic to inherited privilege, and it also lacked a peasantry among whom a socialist view of equality could gain a foothold.[8]

The United States also provided a hospitable physical environment for liberalism. A huge territory with great expanses of

6. Lakoff, *Equality*, p. 127.
7. Locke, "Essay . . . Civil Government," chap. 5, para. 49.
8. This general message is contained in Hartz, *Liberal Tradition*.

fertile "unclaimed" land approximated the conditions of Locke's agrarian liberalism. It was a nation in which the yeoman farmer, protected only by assurances of equal rights, could thrive, and where inequality among (white) persons could be attributed to diligence and skill (aided, of course, by the whims of fortune). It was not until the end of the nineteenth century that the closing of the frontier, exploitation of industrial workers, and evidence of the corrupting power of concentrated wealth produced challenges to liberal doctrine. But even then responses had to come from the liberal tradition itself, because there were no alternative philosophical traditions from which to draw solutions.[9]

Thus while much of the world has long argued, voted, and revolted in favor of leveling gross disparities in wealth, the United States has accepted substantive inequality. As a substitute for equality of result we have placed equality of process—equal protection and equal opportunity. If Americans can convince themselves that the procedure is fair, they believe that the outcome, however unequal, is also fair—that it is related to personal qualities, or at any rate is necessary for increased productivity and economic growth.[10] John Schaar has phrased it most succinctly: Equality in America means giving everyone an equal chance to become unequal.[11]

Since we know that the liberal view of equality is designed to produce inequality among individuals, it is tempting to infer that liberal equality will also produce inequality among racial or ethnic groups. The temptation to draw this inference is strengthened by what we know about limitations on upward mobility. However, such an inference is logically unsound. It requires us to commit the individualist fallacy of assuming that what is true of individuals is also true of groups. Further, such an inference contradicts the conventional wisdom about the ef-

9. Ibid., especially chap. 10.

10. David Potter, *People of Plenty* (Chicago: University of Chicago Press, 1954), especially chap. 4.

11. John Schaar, "Some Ways of Thinking about Equality," *Journal of Politics* 26 (November 1964): 867–95.

fect of equal treatment on ethnic groups in the United States. Those groups, we are told, have achieved economic status roughly on a par with older immigrant groups from England and Northern Europe. And we are led to expect that other groups—blacks, Puerto Ricans, and so on—will realize the same gains once discrimination against them is ended. At best, then, our insights about the effects of liberal equality for individuals alert us to the possibility that equal treatment will produce or perpetuate substantive inequality between the races.

DEFINITION OF EQUAL OPPORTUNITY

There are actually two forms of equal treatment in the United States. One is equal protection, which is mandated by the Fourteenth Amendment.[12] The other, which most concerns us here, is equal opportunity. Equal protection refers to rights. Rights are a peculiar sort of good in that they are not scarce. Everyone can be given the right to vote, and everyone can exercise that right.

Equal opportunity, on the other hand, refers to scarce goods—jobs, housing, education. One can discern the differences between the two forms of equal treatment by noticing how they are used in everyday discourse. We speak of voting rights or the right of free speech or the right to a trial by jury. On the other hand, we talk about equal housing opportunity, equal employment opportunity. We do not say that everyone has a right to a job or a right to enter law school. We say that everyone has an opportunity—or we prescribe that persons be given equal opportunity—to obtain these things.

12. Section 1 reads: "All persons born or naturalized in the United States, and subject to the jurisdiction thereof, are citizens of the United States and of the State wherein they reside. No State shall make or enforce any law which shall abridge the privileges or immunities of citizens of the United States; nor shall any State deprive any person of life, liberty, or property, without due process of law; nor deny any person within its jurisdiction the equal protection of the laws."

Equal opportunity has a structure quite different from that of equal protection. If A and B both want to vote they can both exercise that right, and equal protection guarantees that they be given that right provided they satisfy certain minimal requirements. But if both A and B apply for the same job, or if they both apply for one vacant spot in a medical school, they cannot both receive the good. What equal opportunity means is that both A and B have the same a priori probability of receiving the good. Put differently, it means that certain factors such as race, religion, and sex cannot be used to bias outcomes.

So far, what I have said should not be surprising or objectionable. I have simply said what "everybody" knows—that equal opportunity gives everyone the same chance. (There is a large *ceteris paribus* here, having to do with skills and discrimination that bias chances in real life, but I will deal with that later.) What is important is that this definition, simple and unsurprising as it is, allows us to make statements about the relationship between equal opportunity and some result. It allows us to determine whether equal opportunity is an open or closed rule.

It is not adequate as currently phrased, though. In order to continue, we must translate our common-sense definition into more elegant, formal language: *Equal opportunity means that, given some scarce indivisible good, x, and N persons wanting x, the probability that any person will get x, is 1/N.* So phrased, equal opportunity takes the form of fair, simple game of chance.[13] Then we can understand the distributional effects of the rule by looking at the distributional effects of a game of pure chance. Flipping coins is such a game.[14]

13. "Fair" means that the probability of winning any given flip is not influenced by whether one has won a previous flip "Simple" means that the gains are the same on each round. Both these assumptions contradict the real world phenomenon of cumulativeness; one's chances of getting y are improved if one has already won x, and y is likely to be a bigger stake. I omit cumulativeness in order to simplify presentation.

14. Concealed in the term "distribution" are three analytically dis-

Imagine a fair, simple game of chance played by two teams of 100 each, arranged so that each player from group A flips against someone in group B—A_1 against B_1, A_j against B_j, and so on. Assuming each pair flips a coin, say, 100 times, we can make some statements about the distribution of wins and losses. We are especially interested in the following two questions:

1. At the nth toss, what is likely to be the distribution of wins and losses between any randomly selected pair of competitors (A_i, B_i)?[15] The answer can be described as a bell-shaped curve which peaks at 50 percent. For any randomly selected pair of contestants, the greatest probability is that they will come out even; that is, each will win one-half of the total tosses engaged in by the pair, or $n/2$. (I assume that the players are not risking their own resources, but are competing for goods provided by some outside source. A game of this structure corresponds roughly to a real-life situation in which there is economic growth and free education.)

However, for any member of the pair, the probability distribution ranges from 0 to 100, which means that there is a chance, however small, that one player in the pair will win every toss. Now, since the greatest expectation is that the players will break even, it seems fair to describe any deviation from this expectation as a redistribution. In other words, a game of chance played a finite number of times allows for the possibility of some redistribution between any randomly selected pair of players. In the real world this redistribution may be called "social mobility"; at the end of the game one player is relatively better off, and the other is relatively worse off, compared to where they were when the game began. (See figure 14.)

tinct ideas. First, the term is used in a statistical sense. A second use has to do with the final result of a process; here it is synonymous with "global distribution." A third usage denotes an intermediate step or process; here it is synonymous with "allocation" and "marginal distribution." I have tried to make clear the different usages in the text.

15. I wish to thank Chris Achen, Joe Hauska, and Ed Pauley for instructing me in the esoterica of probability theory.

FIGURE 14.   Frequency Distribution for Individuals
of a Specific, Divisible Good

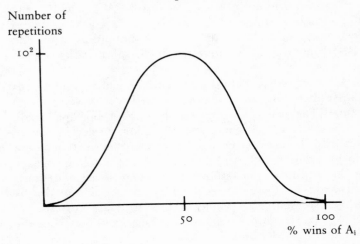

This tells us that, for individuals, the relationship between a rule of equal opportunity and a substantive result is *probabilistically open*. From the rule, we cannot infer results for A_j and B_j. They may come out roughly even; they may not.

2. The second question is, after the nth repetition, what will be the distribution of wins and losses between group A and group B? For large groups engaged in a large number of repetitions, the curve approaches a straight line at 50 percent. (At infinity, the curve is a straight line at 50 percent.) Thus, while individual players may experience redistribution, the probability of redistribution between groups is very small. In the aggregate, individuals' runs of luck cancel out. (See figure 15.)

In other words, when large groups are involved the relationship between rule and result is *probabilistically closed*. Further, it is closed in a specifiable way: The share allocated to each group by a rule of equal opportunity will be $(g_i/N)y$, where y denotes the good, g_i is the population of any subgroup, and N is the size of the total population. Clearly, what this means is

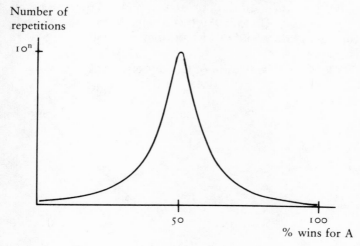

FIGURE 15. Frequency Distribution for Groups of a Specific, Divisible Good

that if the groups are equal at the time the game begins, they will be equal when it ends. If the groups start out unequal, equal opportunity will perpetuate inequality. But let us be more specific.

Assume that at time t_0, A is better off than B; A has goods valued at $m + n$, and B has goods valued at m, so that

$$\frac{y_B}{y_A} = \frac{m}{m + n} \text{ and } y_A - y_B = n.$$

This situation is illustrated graphically in figure 16. P_1 is the distribution of goods at t_0. Line OE is the line of perfect equality, where

$$\frac{y_B}{y_A} = 1, \text{ and } y_A - y_B = 0.$$

Over a time period t_0 to t_1, goods valued at $2w$ are allocated to A and B. The allocation will be Pareto optimizing: No group will be worse off at t_1 than at t_0, and at least one group will be better off. The constraint conforms to two assumptions —economic growth, and no risk of original goods.

FIGURE 16.   Distribution of Goods between A and B at t_0

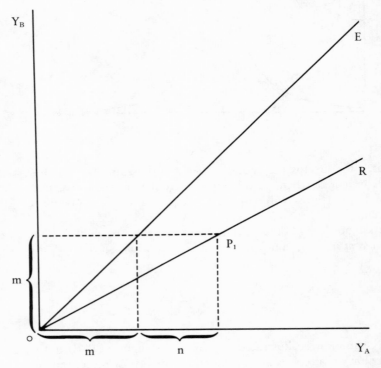

We can now describe both allocations that conform to the distributional effects of equal opportunity and allocations that do not. The text is illustrated by figure 17.

1. If the rule of equal opportunity is followed, goods valued at w would be allocated to both groups at t_1. In figure

FIGURE 17. Pareto-Optimizing Changes in the Distribution of
Goods between A and B

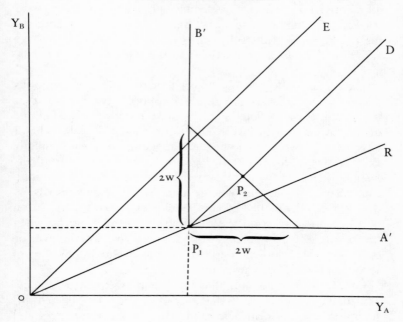

17, movement would be from P_1 to P_2 on line P_1D. Since w_A
$= w_B > 0$, the relative disparity is reduced:

$$\frac{m + w}{m + n + w} > \frac{m}{m + n}$$

However, the absolute difference remains n, as is illustrated by
the fact that P_2 lies on a line parallel to, but below, the line of
perfect equality. Following criteria established in chapter 2, we
can say that this movement represents *ambiguous change*. Our
conclusion: If groups are unequal at the time a rule of equal
opportunity is imposed, the rule will produce ambiguous
change. The reason is obvious. Equal opportunity applies only
to marginal allocations. With respect to marginal allocations,

equal opportunity will produce equal results. However, equal opportunity does nothing to correct past inequality. To put it differently: For large groups, equal opportunity is closed with respect to marginal allocations. But it is open with respect to the total or global distribution of goods. In our society large amounts of goods are not subject to the rule of equal opportunity.

The reader will probably object that this exercise overlooks the most important aspect of equal opportunity, which is that it prescribes awarding goods on the basis of skill or qualifications. But in fact I have not overlooked skill. What I have done is to assume that the competing groups are equally skilled. Where equally skilled groups compete, short-run differences in results will be caused by chance; and in the long run, chance deviations average out. So the exercise tells us that, for equally skilled groups, outcomes are t_1, t_2, and so on will depend heavily on the distribution of goods at t_0, when the rule of equal opportunity is imposed. At least this will be the result absent other interventions, for example, payment of reparations, or confiscatory inheritance taxes.

Of course it is possible that the groups will not be equally skilled. It is also possible that the groups will be affected differently by some form of discrimination. Skill differences and discrimination may be treated as forms of bias; they produce outcomes different from those we would expect from a rule of equal opportunity.

In continuing the formal presentation, I shall use the factor, x, to denote bias; it does not matter much what the source of bias is. Whether bias is caused by racial discrimination or educational advantages, the effect will be the same—which means that when we look at outcomes we cannot determine immediately which type of bias has been at work. Incidentally. skill bias incorporates the sorts of factors emphasized by human capital theorists such as Gary Becker and Lester Thurow, as well as the cultural and socioeconomic factors emphasized by Kenneth Clark, James Coleman, Daniel Moynihan, and E. Franklin Frazier.[16]

16. For discussions of returns on human capital investments see

2. If group A receives a higher *absolute* increment, such that

$$w_A(1 + x) > w_B(1 - x),$$

the absolute disparity between A and B will increase:

$$[m + n + w_A(1 + x)] - [m + w_B(1 - x)] > m + n - m.$$

In figure 17, the new distribution will lie within arc DP_1A'.

3. If group B receives an increment which is higher proportionately but lower absolutely than A, such that

$$\frac{w_B(1 - x)}{m} > \frac{w_A(1 + x)}{m + n}$$

the ratio will close, the new outcome will lie within arc DP_1R. Notice that although the ratio closes, the absolute gap increases. This constitutes ambiguous change.

4. If A and B receive the same proportionate increase, such that

---

Gary Becker, *Human Capital* (New York: Columbia University Press, 1964), esp. pp. 94–100; Lester Thurow, *Investment in Human Capital* (Belmont, Calif.: Wadsworth, 1970); Giora Hanoch, "An Economic Analysis of Earnings and Schooling," *Journal of Human Resources* 2 (Summer 1967): 310–29; Randall Weiss, "The Effects of Education on the Earnings of Blacks and Whites," *Review of Economics and Statistics* 52 (May 1970): 150–59; and Finis Welch, "Black-White Differences in Returns to Schooling," *American Economic Review* 63 (December 1973): 892–97. Researchers tend to agree that black returns on education are smaller than for whites; hence blacks have less incentive to invest. As Althauser and Spivack found, blacks must secure more impressive credentials than whites. See Robert Althauser et al., *The Unequal Elites* (New York: Wiley, 1975). The cultural and scoioeconomic factors are discussed in Kenneth Clark, *Dark Ghetto: Dilemmas of Social Power* (New York: Harper & Row, 1965); James Coleman, *Equality of Educational Opportunity* (Washington: GPO, 1966); E. Franklin Frazier, *The Negro Family in the United States* (Chicago: University of Chicago Press, 1939); and Daniel Moynihan, "The Negro Family: The Case for National Action," in Lee Rainwater and William Yancey, *The Moynihan Report and the Politics of Controversy* (Cambridge: MIT Press, 1967).

$$\frac{w_B(1-x)}{m} > \frac{w_A(1+x)}{m+n}$$

the new distribution will lie along line P_1R. The ratio remains constant, but the absolute gap increases; this is ambiguous change.

5. If A receives an increment proportionately greater than that received by B, such that

$$\frac{w_A(1+x)}{m+n} > \frac{w_B(1-x)}{m}$$

the outcome will lie in arc RP_1A'. Such movement corresponds to our criterion of disequalization as described in chapter 2.

6. If and only if the marginal allocation favors B, such that B receives an increment absolutely greater than that received by A, will there be unambiguous movement toward equality between groups. In figure 17, such movement would lie north of line P_1D.

Application to the problem of inequality between races is fairly straightforward. Equal opportunity, if it existed, would mean that for every substantive gain whites make, blacks could be expected to make the same gain (relative to population, of course). If the races are unequal to begin with, that is, at the time when bias is eliminated, substantive inequality will persist. The most we can expect from equal opportunity is ambiguous change.

But even this discouraging prognosis must be qualified. The United States has at best a form of *weak* biased opportunity. Not all allocations are subject to the rule of equal opportunity. Most jobs and skills are subject to the rule, but many other goods are not. Wealth and unearned income from wealth— interest, rents, dividends—are not covered by the rule. These goods can be passed along intergenerationally, thus perpetuating past advantages. The reader will recall two points from chapter 2: On average, whites hold considerably more wealth than blacks; and whites hold forms of wealth that appreciate more rapidly.

Further, the allocation of goods is biased; equal opportunity for the races simply does not exist yet. One type of bias, racial discrimination, may diminish over time, but there is considerable evidence that it persists today.[17] Another type derives from the financial and cultural advantages enjoyed by whites. It is not clear how much this type of bias can be reduced without drastic interventions. I shall argue later that affirmative action attempts to deal with one of these forms of bias.

Our conclusion must be that the form of equal opportunity practiced in America will serve to perpetuate racial inequality. Pure equal opportunity, if it could be achieved, would produce ambiguous change and allow some racial inequality to persist. But in reality we have weak opportunity combined with bias; so we may expect worse results. The disequalization that occurred in the early 1970s tends to confirm this expectation.

UNEMPLOYMENT

I propose now to apply this understanding of equal opportunity to the persistent and perplexing problem of unemployment. Chapter 2 indicated that black and white employment rates tend to move in the same direction, and that the black unemployment rate remains about double the white rate.

If equal opportunity applied to employment, then we would expect that for every z percent change in the white unemploy-

17. See for example Althauser and Spivack, *Unequal Elites*; Otis Dudley Duncan, "Inheritance of Poverty or Inheritance of Race?" in *On Understanding Poverty*, ed. Daniel Moynihan (New York: Basic Books, 1968); George von Furstenburg, Ann Horowitz, and Bennett Harrison, *Patterns of Racial Discrimination*, 2 vols. (Lexington, Mass.: Lexington Books, 1974); Stanley Masters, *Black-White Income Differentials* (New York: Academic Press, 1975); and Gerald Scully, "Discrimination: The Case of Baseball," in *Government and the Sports Business*, ed. Roger Noll (Washington: Brookings, 1974). See also, "U.S. Courts in the South Are Accused of Job Bias," *The Washington Post*, October 11, 1978, p. A8; and Stacy Jolna, "Bias in Home Financing Based on Race," *The Washington Post*, December 8, 1978, p. A4.

ment rate, there would be a z percent change in the black unemployment rate. Let us apply this rule to a situation in which whites have an unemployment rate of x and blacks have an unemployment rate of $x + y$. These predictions follow:

1. As the overall unemployment rate increases, the ratio of black to white unemployment decreases.

$$\frac{x + y}{x} > \frac{x + y + z}{x + z}$$

2. As the overall unemployment rate decreases, the ratio of black to white unemployment increases.

$$\frac{x + y}{x} < \frac{x + y - z}{x - z}$$

These conclusions are illustrated in figure 18. The axes represent percentage of each race unemployed. P is the unemployment rate at t_0. Line OR, which passes through P, indicates a constant ratio of black to white unemployment. Line CD, which runs through P and is parallel to the line of equal unemployment, OE, marks the effect of equal opportunity starting from P. It is clear that line sector PD is north of the constant ratio line, thus indicating that as unemployment increases, the black/white ratio "improves." Likewise, segment CP is south of OR, indicating a growing ratio as overall unemployment decreases. The slope of line CD indicates that if perfect equal opportunity exists in employment the absolute gap in unemployment rates between black and white cohorts will remain constant.

What this suggests is that lessening the black/white unemployment differential requires more than merely reducing overall unemployment and ensuring equal opportunity. Rather, it requires hiring blacks at a faster rate than whites during periods of rapid growth, and laying blacks off at a slower rate during periods of economic slowdown. This is exactly the opposite of past and current practices. As a result of bias and of senior-

FIGURE 18.   Effects of Changes in Black and White
Unemployment Rates

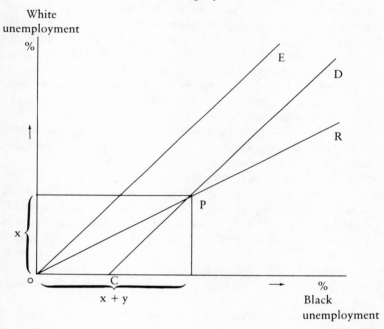

ity systems that tend to perpetuate the effects of past discrimination, blacks continue to suffer disproportionately during periods of layoff and are the last to benefit from growth.[18]

18. When I interviewed officials at the Equal Employment Opportunity Commission in 1975, I was told that blacks seemed no longer
to be suffering the last hired, first fired syndrome. As evidence,
officials cited the black/white unemployment ratio, which did not increase during the 1974–75 recession. However, the exercise above suggests that the ratio is not sensitive enough to gauge whether blacks are
being laid off at a disproportionately high rate. Since the ratio is nor-
mally around 2 to 1, it will increase only if the black layoff rate is
more than twice the white layoff rate. The very egregiousness of current
inequality serves to conceal lesser inequities.

Affirmative Action

I will concentrate here on the more controversial aspects of affirmative action, those practices that give rise to polemics about reverse discrimination, quotas, and threats to the "merit system." Other aspects of affirmative action, for example requirements that jobs be advertised rather than whispered over an "old boy network," seem to generate little controversy.

The parts of affirmative action that produce the greatest outcry are those designed to answer the following questions: (1) How can we tell when discrimination has occurred? and (2) What can we do about the persisting effects of past discrimination? After addressing these I shall take up some of the criticisms of affirmative action, including the tired complaint that it requires employers to hire the unqualified.

1. Suppose a situation in which racial discrimination is an accepted, common, and legal practice. In such a situation, it would probably be easy to tell whether an employer practiced discrimination. We could ask him, and if he did, he would probably tell us the truth. But suppose racial discrimination is made illegal. Is it now reasonable to expect complete compliance; and is it reasonable to expect an employer to admit noncompliance?

Earlier I cited evidence that discrimination persists. Some of the evidence is derived from statistical methods. When other sources of bias—education and skills—are controlled for, a gap between black and white earned income remains. It is reasonable to infer that discrimination accounts for much of the remaining gap. Statistical evidence is supplemented by myriad concrete instances of persisting discrimination.

Unfortunately, the procedures originally implemented to deal with discrimination were inadequate. Before the more stringent affirmative action procedures were implemented, each aggrieved individual had to prove that an employer had discriminated against him, even when the employer in question had a history of discriminating. In case-by-case litigation the burden of proof could be very heavy. For example, the plaintiff may have had to show that he was more qualified for a position than the person hired to fill it. Showing that he was equally qualified would be insufficient. For when applicants are equally qualified, the employer could well decide among them by flipping coins.

(Let me elaborate the last statement. Suppose that, whenever a personnel officer is forced to choose between equally qualified black and white applicants, he flips a coin. This is a totally "objective" procedure. It is possible that whites will win consistently, but this could not be said to constitute discrimination. Of course it is also possible that blacks will win consistently, and this could not be called "reverse discrimination.")

Aside from the odious burden of proof placed on the plaintiff, the procedures for redress could be ludicrously inefficient and time-consuming. The Equal Employment Opportunity Commission alone had a backlog of ninety thousand complaints in 1975.[19] Surely there was some way to avoid the discouraging ineffectiveness of the old procedures without imposing quotas indiscriminately or assuming that every employer was guilty of discrimination. One solution was simply to shift the burden of proof from the minority worker to the employer, union, or job referral agency in question. Affirmative action allows that to be done in situations where minorities are flagrantly underrepresented in a work force. Such underrepresentation can be taken as prima facie evidence (not proof) of discrimination—evidence that an employer can be asked to refute.[20]

Shifting the burden of proof to the employer is not tanta-

19. "An Industry Man Takes Over a Battered EEOC," *Business Week*, June 23, 1975, pp. 113–15.
20. "Beyond the *Prima Facie* Case in Employment Discrimination Law: Statistical Proof and Rebuttal," *Harvard Law Review* 89 (December 1975): 387–422. My interpretation of the background of affirmative action is generally consistent with positions taken by the U.S. Commission on Civil Rights in its *Statement on Affirmative Action* (Washington: GPO, 1977). I wish to thank Chairman Arthur Flemming for bringing this publication to my attention. However, I am not sure that Dr. Flemming would support my projections about the limited effects of affirmative action.

mount to assuming that every employer is guilty of discrimination, any more than placing the burden of proof on the plaintiff
is tantamount to assuming that every unsuccessful job applicant
is unqualified. However, in view of the history of discrimination in the United States, and ample evidence that it persists, it
seems to me that the burden of proof has been placed appropriately. It simply makes sense to assume that, absent vigilant and
forceful intervention, old prejudices and practices will reassert
themselves, although perhaps in subtle ways.

Further, employers are better able to bear the burden of
proof than are individual plaintiffs. For one thing, employers
have ready access to necessary resources. One of the problems
with the old procedures was that plaintiffs often had to engage
in protracted struggles merely to get employers to release evidence relevant to a case, such as personnel records and employment policies.[21] When employers bear the burden of proof, they
are more likely to come forward with the necessary evidence.

Absent long-standing and pervasive racial discrimination, we
would expect the races to be similar in socioeconomic status.
This does not mean, of course, that we would expect exactly 11
percent of avocado farmers or psychiatrists to be black. But
there are examples of black underrepresentation in some trades
and professions that even the most shrill critics of affirmative
action must find suspicious. For example, in Washington,
D.C., in the late 1960s, fewer than 2 percent of sheet-metal
workers and none of the city's boilermakers were black.[22] Such
disproportions, which investigation revealed to be the result of
discrimination, caused enforcement agencies to impose hiring
guidelines on the offending unions. In Philadelphia, several unions had virtually no black members. The original Philadelphia
Plan imposed hiring guidelines on only six unions, those having
less than 2 percent black membership.[23]

21. In *E.E.O.C.* v. *University of New Mexico* (10th Cir. 1974), the
court ordered the employer to release confidential employment records to the equal Employment Opportunity Commission so that the
agency could investigate a complaint.
22. Code of Federal Regulations, title 41, chap. 60. sec. 5.11.
23. Peter Nash, "Affirmative Action under Executive Order 11246,"
New York University Law Review 46 (1971): 225–61.

Many cases are not so clear-cut, of course. Enforcement agencies and the courts must decide when the proportion of black workers is flagrantly low in relation to the numbers of qualified blacks available. Obviously there can be no single standard. It would be futile to search for a precise definition of "underutilization" which will work equally well for a Boston bricklayers' union and a university faculty. Such determinations must be made locally and take account of the area's racial composition, employment market, and the type of training necessary for specific jobs. Contrary to the view espoused by their opponents, affirmative action plans do not consist of uniform quotas that fatuous Washington bureaucrats impose on hapless, well-intentioned employers.[24] Rather, they result from a complex and time-consuming process of fact-finding, legal maneuvering, and political bargaining at the local level. The Equal Employment Opportunity Commission is required by law to allow local agencies (where they exist) to handle complaints.[25]

Under affirmative action then, the first question is answered as follows: Certain statistical measures can be used as prima facie evidence of discrimination. Where such prima facie evidence exists, the burden of proof can be shifted to the employer. When the employer fails to carry the burden of proof, some redress is in order. Redress may include hiring guidelines or quotas, and back pay for employees who have suffered discrimination in layoffs or promotions.

This approach to finding and redressing discrimination is intrusive. It often requires employers to keep records and file reports that they might ordinarily not do. And it requires them to be more aggressive in recruiting minorities than they would ordinarily be. No doubt, then, afiirmative action involves procedures and costs that employers would rather not bear. However, the measures are necessary because experience demonstrates that many employers continue to practice discrimination. And the alternative, case-by-case litigation, would

24. For one polemicist's shrill complaint, see Nathan Glazer, *Affirmative Discrimination: Ethnic Inequality and Public Policy* (New York: Basic Books, 1975).
25. *Code of Federal Regulations*, title 29, chap. 14, sec. 1601.12.

probably be far more costly, inefficient, and time-consuming. The original affirmative action guidelines, contained in Executive Order 11246, merely called on employers to act in "good faith" to satisfy antidiscrimination laws. Unfortunately, it soon became clear that large numbers of employers would not act in good faith, so more stringent measures became necessary. The Comptroller General demanded numerical guidelines, because the "good faith" standard was simply too vague to be used as a standard for judging compliance with the law.[26]

2. A second problem addressed by affirmative action involves ostensibly neutral rules that perpetuate the effects of past discrimination. Seniority systems can do this. A classic example came to light in *United Papermakers* v. *United States*.[27] Blacks had long been restricted to the lowest paying departments at the plant, and the 1964 Civil Rights Act made it possible for them to demand transfers to better paying departments. However, seniority at the plant was based on length of service in a specific department, so blacks who requested transfers were subject to loss of income and seniority. A federal judge wrote the following about this instance of the continuing effects of past discrimination:

The defendants assert, paradoxically, that even though the system conditions future employment opportunities upon a previously determined racial status the system is itself racially neutral and is not in violation of Title VII. The translation of racial status to job seniority status cannot obscure the hard, cold fact that Negroes at Crown's mill lose promotions which, *but for* their race, they would surely have won. Every time a Negro worker hired under the old segregated system bids against a white worker in his job slot, the old racial classification reasserts itself, and the Negro suffers anew for his employer's previous bias.[28]

26. Earl Leiken, "Preferential Treatment in the Skilled Building Trades: An Analysis of the Philadelphia Plan," *Cornell Law Review* 56 (1970): 84–113.

27. *United Papermakers and Paperworkers, Local 189*, v. *United States*, 416 F.2d 980 (5th Cir. 1969), cert. denied, 397 U.S. 191 (1970).

28. 416 F.2d at 988.

Where seniority systems perpetuate the effects of past discrimination, the courts and enforcement agencies may impose affirmative remedies such as adjustments of seniority systems, conversion to plant-wide seniority systems, and red-lining pay schedules so that blacks who request transfers will not suffer income loss. The remedies place blacks in positions they would have occupied but for discrimination. In this sense, affirmative action merely imposes the results one could expect from equal opportunity. Therefore, it is difficult to argue that affirmative action favors blacks. Quite the contrary: It simply imposes equal opportunity on an environment pervaded by bias.

Certain types of job qualifications can also perpetuate the effects of past discrimination. Suppose employers will hire only high school graduates in a state where blacks are usually denied access to a high school education. It is obvious that such a requirement will have the effect, if not the purpose, of discriminating against blacks. It is also obvious that equalizing future black and white educational opportunities will not benefit blacks currently seeking employment. Their fate has been fixed by the combination of past discrimination and current "neutral" rules.

The Supreme Court has ruled that the 1964 Civil Rights Act

proscribes not only overt discrimination but also practices that are fair in form, but discriminatory in operation. The touchstone is business necessity. If an employment practice which operates to exclude Negroes cannot be shown to be related to job performance, the practice is prohibited.[29]

It is clear from this and similar rulings that neither the courts nor enforcement agencies wish to deprive employers of the right to set minimal qualifications for employees. However, where such qualifications have discriminatory effect, they will be scrutinized closely. If they are not related to the jobs employees are expected to perform, they may be proscribed.

29. *Griggs* v. *Duke Power Company*, 401 U.S. 424 (1971).

Affirmative action helps reduce racial bias in the allocation of goods by providing an efficient way to identify current discrimination and providing means to mediate the persisting effects of past discrimination. However, it cannot eliminate legitimate skill bias.[30]

3. Unobjectionable as its purposes appear, affirmative action has been subjected to considerable criticism. Below I address two objections—that affirmative action is illegal, and that it sets aside merit criteria and requires blacks be given preferential treatment.

Some critics charge that affirmative action is illegal, whatever its other merits. Specifically, detractors claim that the 1964 Civil Rights Act prohibits some of the affirmative action procedures now in force. The claim appears compelling because the 1964 act does indeed preclude "preferential treatment to any individual or to any group because of race, color, religion, sex, or national origin."[31] However, that clause represents only a portion of the relevant law. The Civil Rights Act allows courts to require those guilty of discrimination to engage in "such affirmative action as may be appropriate which may include the reinstatement or hiring of employees, with or without back pay."[32] This section was strengthened in the 1972 Equal Employment Opportunity Act. A court finding discrimination may "order such affirmative action as may be appropriate which may include, but it is not limited to, reinstatement or hiring of employees, with or without back pay . . . *or any other equitable relief* as the court deems appropriate."[33] What this means is that, absent a finding of discrimination, the courts and enforcement agencies may run afoul of the law if they impose hiring guidelines or quotas. But where there is a finding of discrimination, such remedies are in order.

30. There is, of course, considerable controversy over the definition of "business necessity" and over what it means to be "qualified." The meaning of business necessity is amplified in *Robinson* v. *Lorillard Corporation*, 444 F.2d 791 (4th Cir. 1971).

31. Title VII, sec. 703(j).

32. Title VII, sec. 706(g).

33. Title VII, sec. 706(g), as amended. Emphasis added.

I must note, however, that there are inconsistencies and ambiguities in the 1964 act and in the 1972 amendments. For example, Section 703(h) endorses "a bona fide seniority . . . system." But Congress left it to the courts to decide whether a seniority system that perpetuates the effects of past discrimination could be considered bona fide.[34] In my view, a seniority system or any other rule that perpetuates the effects of discrimination is presumptively unjust.

Two recent Supreme Court decisions support affirmative action in principle, but perpetuate ambiguity with respect to specifics. In the celebrated *Bakke* case, the Court decided, by a 5 to 4 majority, that the system used by the University of California-Davis Medical School to admit minorities was impermissible.[35] By an equally narrow margin, a different majority decided that race could be considered in admissions decisions. Three key facts about the Cal-Davis plan: (a) It was voluntary, not enacted to compensate for past discrimination by the university. (b) It was based on explicit quotas. Sixteen of 100 places in the entering class were reserved for minorities. Whites could not compete for the sixteen reserved seats, but minorities could compete for the unreserved seats, and several did so successfully. (c) None of the minority students admitted was unqualified, although, on average, those admitted under the special program had lower "objective" scores than regular applicants.

Justice Powell, who provided the pivot vote for both majorities, cited a Harvard College program as an example of the type of program that would be acceptable. The major dif-

---

34. See *United Papermakers* v. *United States*, but also the Supreme Court's recent rulings in *Teamsters* v. *United States*, No. 75-636, and *T.I.M.E.-D.C. Inc.* v. *United States*, No. 75-672. Decisions will turn on the following two issues: first, whether the courts will consider the continuing effects of discriminatory acts that occurred before the 1964 Act went into effect, or only acts that occurred after the effective date of the Act; second, whether the courts focus on discriminatory intent or discriminatory effect.

35. *Regents of the University of California* v. *Bakke*, No. 76-811. (June 28, 1978), 46 LW 4896.

ference between the Cal-Davis program and the Harvard program is explicitness. Harvard does not use quotas; but it does use race to break ties.

As if to reinforce its affirmative opinion, a few days after *Bakke* the Supreme Court denied certiorari to appeals in which three unions challenged an American Telephone and Telegraph (AT&T) affirmative action plan.[36] The plan was initiated in 1973 following a consent decree; it involved specific targets for women and minorities; and it overrode seniority "rights."

While both cases support affirmative action, differences between them raise questions about the subsidiary messages the Court wishes to convey. It may be saying: (a) that a consent decree carries obligations severe enough to justify specific targets and overrule other obligations, such as seniority rights; (b) that affirmative action in employment will be viewed differently from affirmative action in college admissions; (c) that goals or targets are different from quotas, and that targets are permissible.

Regardless of the Court's explicit support for certain forms of affirmative action, the *Bakke* decision may have a chilling effect. For reasons genuine or cynical, universities and employers are beginning to reassess their affirmative action programs. At least one law school has abolished its minority admissions committee. And AT&T, one of the country's largest employers, will probably reduce its affirmative action efforts when its consent decree expires in 1979.[37]

My response to the second objection, that affirmative action sets aside merit criteria and requires that blacks be given preferential treatment, will look first at the law on this point and next at the meaning of preferential treatment. The law is quite clear: Employers may set employment qualifications and may

36. *Communications Workers of America* v. E.E.O.C., No. 77–241, cert. denied (July 3, 1978); CA3, 45 LW 2508.

37. See Jack Egon, "Changes May Be Needed in AT&T Hiring Program," *The Washington Post*, July 4, 1978; Alice Bonner, "Schools Taking A Second Look at Affirmative Action," *The Washington Post*, December 7, 1978.

use tests or other devices to measure qualifications.[38] But a thoughtful person would grant that Congress never intended to approve the use of *any* test. Surely it intended to license only tests with some relevance to the job an applicant was expected to perform. And so the Supreme Court has ruled; the landmark case is *Griggs* v. *Duke Power Company*.[39]

The case questioned whether an employer could require a high school diploma or a certain score on a general intelligence test as a qualification for employment. The qualifications appear innocuous. Unfortunately, because blacks in North Carolina had received inferior education in segregated schools, they tended to suffer disproportionately from the requirements. (Interestingly, the employer enacted the more stringent requirements on the day Title VII became effective; but the Supreme Court did not find discriminatory intent.)

The Court ruled that tests having racially discriminatory effects must be related to "business necessity"—to the jobs applicants must perform. Conversely, qualifications that satisfy the business necessity criterion are permissible, even if they have discriminatory effects. The merit system remains intact.

Congress did not intend by Title VII . . . to guarantee a job to every person regardless of qualification. . . . What is required by Congress is the removal of artificial, arbitrary, and unnecessary barriers to employment when the barriers operate invidiously to discriminate on the basis of racial or other impermissible classification.[40]

Further, the use of guidelines or quotas need not involve preferential treatment, if by preferential treatment we mean some violation of merit criteria. To clarify this we can examine what preferential treatment means in practice. Suppose an employer insists a job be filled by a high school graduate, and persons with the following educational qualifications apply: (a)

38. This was set forth in Title VII, sec. 703(h) of the 1964 Civil Rights Act and in the 1972 amendments.

39. 401 U.S. 424 (1971).

40. *Griggs* v. *Duke Power Company*, 401 U.S. at 427.

someone who has completed only ten years of school; (b) a high school graduate; (c) a college graduate; (d) a Ph.D. If the employer hires the applicant who has not completed high school and rejects others, I think we could accuse him of preferential treatment because he has chosen someone who does not meet his minimal qualifications. (Whether the qualifications are required by business necessity need not concern us here). But if he hires the high school graduate and rejects the Ph.D., is he guilty of preferential treatment? This is not obvious, since both are qualified by minimal criteria. My point here is that hiring a black instead of a white can be called preferential treatment only if the black is unqualified and the white qualified. (The opposite also applies, of course.)

It may be objected that strict application of merit criteria requires that an employer hire the most highly qualified, rather than simply choosing among applicants who satisfy minimal criteria. This may be true in theory but one doubts that it applies in practice. Consider the U.S. Civil Service system, which ostensibly applies vigorous merit criteria. The Civil Service is not required automatically to hire the person who, by its reckoning, is most qualified. Rather, it practices a "rule of three": It chooses among several highly ranked applicants. Further, the federal government's "merit system" includes factors that even its most ardent supporters must regard as embarrassing irrelevancies—military service, seniority, and apportionment rules that place persons from urban areas at a competitive disadvantage. In effect, if not by design, the merit system is a set of preference rules weighted in favor of white males.

My guess is that most employers use wide discretion in choosing among applicants. Indeed, I suggest that the designation "most qualified" is applied after a hiring decision is made. Before the fact, employers (and deans of admission) have only the vaguest idea what the "most qualified" applicant would look like. It is tempting to resort to strict numerical solutions—scores on tests. But very few employers are willing to rely solely on such measures.

Further, a true merit system implies open competition for all positions, so that when an employer finds an applicant who is better qualified than the current holder of a position, the current employee is replaced. But seniority systems, tenure, and closed shops serve to diminish competition. If opponents of affirmative action are really concerned about threats to the merit system, they should channel their energies toward eliminating institutional safeguards against competition.

Regardless of the truth about affirmative action, its opponents have succeeded in biasing opinion against it. For example, a recent Gallup poll revealed that a vast majority of persons reject affirmative action.[41] But an informed reading of the poll shows why. In essence, the survey asks, "Do you believe minorities ought to be given preferential treatment, or should hiring be based on ability?" The results are not surprising, given the way the question is posed. And given what we now know about affirmative action, the pollster is guilty either of disingenuousness or ignorance. For in truth there is no conflict between affirmative action and hiring based on ability.

Now suppose an employer or admissions dean enacts a decision rule which states, "Given a choice between a qualified black and a qualified white, I will select the black." Based on Justice Powell's comments on Harvard College's program, I think that the Supreme Court would be tolerant of such a rule if it were phrased and used judiciously.[42] The employer or college would have to make a convincing claim that blacks bring to the job or the school a diversity of perspective otherwise lacking. By Powell's lights, of course, similar claims could be made about geographic origin, at least with regard to college.

The controversial aspects of affirmative action developed in response to two problems—the difficulty of case-by-case litigation, and the need to mitigate persisting effects of past discrimination. It does not violate merit criteria by requiring employers

41. "Poll Slap at Affirmative Action," *San Francisco Chronicle*, May 2, 1977, p. 4.
42. *Bakke*, 46 LW at 4909.

to hire the unqualified, although it is not surprising that its opponents find this a convenient rhetorical ploy to use against it. It does not violate the law. Nor does it mitigate the effects of skill bias, although it does allow us to demand that the skill bias be related to business necessity.

In short, affirmative action intends at most to ensure weak equal opportunity or to produce the effects one could reasonably expect from weak equal opportunity. Earlier I demonstrated that a rule of weak equal opportunity will, at best, lead to ambiguous change in the standing of the races. It is ironic that such controversy surrounds policies that promise so little. Most of the controversy results from the fact that affirmative action is misunderstood, or purposely misrepresented.

The White Immigrants Analogy

I suspect that many objections to affirmative action are conditioned by a curiously obtuse view of the experiences of white immigrant groups. We are told that these groups were discriminated against when they arrived in the United States, but that over time discrimination eased, so that second- and third-generation immigrants could take advantage of equal treatment to achieve upward mobility. We are led to expect that blacks will replicate the experiences of white ethnics. Given this understanding of United States social history, it is not surprising that many react quite strongly to any suggestion that blacks be given special help or compensatory treatment. The Irish and the Jews did not get special treatment, we are told, so neither should the blacks.[43]

The typical response to this line of argument is empirical. Critics point out that the conditions under which blacks must struggle for success are quite different from the conditions confronting immigrants in the nineteenth and early twentieth centuries. There are no more frontiers to be settled, no cities to be built; economic growth has slowed. Wage competition among individuals has been replaced by job competition replete with

43. This simpleminded view occasionally carries an acceptable academic pedigree. See for example Glazer, *Affirmative Discrimination*.

credentialism, union perquisites, and highly institutionalized hiring procedures.[44] Opportunities for becoming a robber baron, a carpetbagger, or a gunrunner have declined.[45]

I find this type of response enlightening, but hardly definitive. It leads to interminable debates and ill-conceived comparisons: Is a black man seeking a college degree today analogous to an Italian-American seeking basic literacy in 1900? Is it true that Irishmen were once valued less than slaves?[46] How is affirmative action for blacks different from the ethnic arithmetic used to staff the Boston Police Department?

One can respond to the white ethnics ploy without indulging in such debates. The issue is, at base, one of definition and simple logic: In a society permeated by racial discrimination, it makes no sense to say that one group suffers discrimination while another group receives equal treatment. If one group is discriminated *against*, the other group is discriminated *for*.

It may well be true that first-generation Irish (or Italians or Jews or Poles) were discriminated against vis-à-vis older

44. Lester Thruow argues that job competition has replaced wage competition in the American labor market. Under job competition, employers group job applicants according to certain criteria, e.g., level of education. One's chances of getting a job depend on how one ranks on these criteria. Since blacks (and women) are disadvantaged by many criteria, they are at a competitive disadvantage vis-à-vis white males. Further—and this is the significant aspect of the job competition model—employers do not base hiring decisions on consideration of individual merit but on what employers believe about the groups to which applicants belong. Thus a woman is at a disadvantage because, on average, there is more job absenteeism among women as a group. See *Generating Inequality: Mechanisms of Distribution in the U.S. Economy* (New York: Basic Books, 1975), chaps. 4 and 5.

45. Stephen Birmingham, in one of those passages of practiced naivete for which he has become well known, wonders at the fact that blacks did not take advantage of the lucrative extralegal opportunities that produced many white millionaires during the Civil War. See *Certain People* (Boston: Little, Brown, 1977).

46. Thomas Sowell offers an entertaining but unenlightening anecdote on this in *Race and Economics* (New York: David McKay, 1975).

white immigrants. Indeed, at one time or another, each of these groups competed with blacks for jobs and housing. Obviously, the immigrants generally won. For example, in 1862, Irish longshoremen forced the dismissal of all blacks from the New York docks.[47]

But to say that white ethnics eventually were given equal treatment vis-à-vis other whites is to say that they were given favored treatment vis-à-vis blacks. It was favored treatment, not equal treatment, that allowed these groups to advance economically and surpass blacks.

Two points follow. First, if the blacks-as-immigrants analogy is to hold, then blacks must experience favored treatment vis-à-vis some group. Second, this is not what blacks are being offered. Rather, blacks are (grudgingly) being offered mere equal treatment. If whites received special treatment, why should not blacks receive special treatment?

Let me repeat the point, since it is often conveniently overlooked. When we say that blacks were discriminated against, logic compels us to concede the obverse: there has been systematic discrimination in favor of whites. This is what makes current complaints about "reverse discrimination" so hollow and hypocritical.

I do not mean, of course, that every WASP or Italian or Jew owes his current position to favored treatment. I suggest merely that the relative position of groups is influenced heavily by the degree to which they benefited or suffered from discrimination. Other factors operate on groups, of course: selective emigration, selective admission of group members into the United States, and the culture of the group. Within groups, the standing of individuals will be affected by family background, native talent, a host of personality variables, and luck.

47. See Herman D. Bloch, *The Circle of Discrimination: An Economic and Social Study of the Black Man in New York* (New York: New York University Press, 1969); Alban P. Mann, Jr., "Labor Competition and The New York Draft Riots of 1863," *The Journal of Negro History*, 36 (October 1951): 375–405; and William M. Tuttle, Jr., "Labor Conflict and Racial Violence: The Black Worker in Chicago, 1894–1919," *Labor History*, 10 (Summer 1969): 408–32.

If the blacks-as-immigrants ploy is so obviously flawed, one wonders how it developed and why it has persisted. One answer is that most social analysis is written by whites. And from a white perspective the analogy may make sense. One cannot criticize white social scientists for viewing the world through their own racial experience; blacks, Indians, and Asian-Americans do the same. But if we are likely to view the world through the lens of racial experience, we can reduce distortion only by ensuring that the views of all races are represented. By failing to act vigorously to recruit or produce minority scholars, academic institutions help to perpetuate distortion.

Notice, incidentally, that the blacks-as-immigrants ploy involves a curious rewriting of history. It asks us to forget that blacks were a sizable minority in the United States a full two centuries before the hordes of white ethnics began to arrive. Why are blacks now in the position of having to catch up with groups that arrived much later? The answer is clear: by law and social practice, whites have been treated for more generously than blacks. Nothing in the experience of white immigrants can match the three and a half centuries of indignity, repression, and violence suffered by blacks. All this is made worse by the fact that it was perpetrated under sanction of law.[48]

Racial equality can be achieved under a rule of *global equal opportunity*. By global I mean that the rule applies to all goods, not just to a portion of future allocations. By equal opportunity I mean that bias across races has been neutralized or eliminated. A rule of *weak equal opportunity* will lead to racial equality only under one condition: that the races are substantively equal at the time the rule is imposed. Failing that condition, the rule will produce ambiguous change.

Our society currently operates under a rule of *weak biased opportunity*. The rule will produce racial equality if and only if the bias is in favor of the worse-off group. Unfortunately, bias

48. See Mary Frances Berry, *Black Resistance, White Law: A History of Constitutional Racism in America*, Englewood Cliffs, N.J.: (Prentice-Hall, 1971); and A. Leon Higgenbotham, Jr., *In the Matter of Color* (New York: Oxford University Press, 1978).

currently favors the advantaged group. With rapid economic growth and a host of other favorable economic conditions, a rule of weak biased opportunity (with bias in favor of whites) could produce ambiguous change. Failing those favorable conditions, the current rule could lead to disequalization in the standing of blacks relative to whites.

If equal opportunity is to produce racial equality, then it is clear that a period of compensatory inequality is required. This conclusion, unpalatable as it may be, follows inexorably from the analysis advanced in this chapter. It simply makes no sense to pretend that "equal" opportunity, as we now practice it, will lead us toward racial equality.

In a way, equal opportunity turns against itself. It is intended to be an open rule for individuals, one which promises that merit will win out over privilege. But it turns into a closed rule for groups, one which actually protects privilege and perpetuates the effects of past injustice.

5

Conclusion: Beyond the Paradox of Procedural Equality

IN THE PAST THREE DECADES this nation has made significant strides toward equalizing treatment of the races. We have outlawed overt forms of racial discrimination; blacks are excluded from no major sector of American society solely on grounds of race. Those changes were hard won, as the history of protracted legal battles and the list of martyred civil rights leaders will attest.

Nor have the victories been purely procedural. Rare now is the business firm or government agency which does not have at least a few senior-level blacks—people in positions of real influence. Louis Martin, who has served three presidents, remarks on the dramatic changes in government:

> When I first came to Washington to work for President Kennedy, I kept looking around for other blacks. I was virtually alone in the White House in those days. The situation was bleak in the executive agencies, until Robert Weaver became Secretary of Housing and Urban Development. In Congress, there were barely enough black members and staff for a decent poker game, let alone a Black Caucus. Today, things are very different."[1]

Those are encouraging changes, and many blacks who have long experience in government, business, or the professions may second Martin's observations. Yet as I showed in chapter 2, blacks are still sadly underrepresented among executives and professionals. Senior-level blacks are more visible than at any time in the past; but statistically, they remain an anomaly. Even

1. Remarks before a group, including the author, November 15, 1978, Washington, D.C. Quoted with permission.

141

in government, which has a special obligation to ensure that minorities exercise influence and power, it is not unusual to see a meeting of senior bureaucrats where only the perspective of white males is represented.

In chapter 4 I explained how a number of blacks could achieve success and prominence, while the situation of blacks as a group remained unchanged. The elementary statistical exercise in that chapter may fill a void between traditional Marxist and liberal theory. Classic Marxists can explain how blacks as a group remain disadvantaged, but cannot account for the huge successes of large numbers of blacks. Classic liberals can easily explain upward social mobility, but have difficulty addressing the continuing depressed condition of blacks as a group. I have shown how both phenomena can occur simultaneously: under current rules, individuals in a group can experience significant mobility while the position of the group remains relatively unchanged. This is the paradox of procedural equality. While it may help the individual, it threatens to trap blacks as a group into a position of permanent substantive inequality vis-à-vis whites.

Thus we find that the struggle for true racial equality is only partially won. After three hundred years we have erased the stigma of legally sanctioned second-class citizenship. And in the past two decades we have established a legal arsenal to ensure equal treatment for individuals. Now we must turn our attention to the second part of the struggle. We must begin to engage the national conscience and the national will in the pursuit of substantive racial equality. Why, and how?

In chapter 2, I asked the reader to view racial inequality from a perspective of uninformed self interest. I presented representative persons with a scenario: The veil of ingorance will soon be lifted, and you will learn precisely what your place is in the real world. Before that happens, let me present some facts about the world and describe to you how it works, and see how you react.

I then told representative persons about racial inequality and showed how current rules may perpetuate that condition. Representative persons would see racial inequality as highly prob-lematic. Persons who do not know their race would not like their life chances, or the situation of their racial group, limited by factors beyond their control, which have no rational justification and which are directly related to past injustices. They certainly would have no reason to defend race-related entitlements. The person whose judgment is not clouded by specific racial identification would regard some form of cor-rective action as intuitively fair.

Further, even the most racially self-interested white must see some injustice in the past treatment of blacks. And I have shown how past injustice affects present and future conditions. By conventional moral standards, persons and societies are obliged to correct injustice. Failure to do so is simple moral cowardice.

When a society engages in corrective action, it may do so without attributing specific blame. It is not relevant that the current generation never owned slaves, or (to indulge the reductio) that Allan Bakke never personally discriminated against blacks. A society is, by definition, an ongoing entity. From preceding generations we inherit structures and real goods and often greatness; we also inherit problems.

Nor is it relevant that the injustices we all concede occurred, occurred under sanction of law. This is not a narrow legal is-sue; it is a moral one. We have discovered error and the persist-ing effects of error. The question is, do we have the moral cour-age to correct it?

Let me offer an analogy which, by contrast with the current problem, is rather pedestrian. Suppose we discovered that an industrial practice that was common and legal thirty years ago now threatened the health of a large number of people. We could outlaw the practice, but that does not help the victims. Do we have an obligation to move beyond simple injunction, toward some effort to make the victims whole? I believe we do. It is an obligation we incur as members of the society in which the error occurred.

In this sort of situation, our search for a specific blameable party may be misdirected. Even if we could identify the malefactors responsible, I am not sure we would want to demand that they bear total responsibility for compensating the victims. They were, after all, following accepted practice at the time. Also, in this situation, I accept that I would pay part of the compensation. It would be rather silly for me to protest that I am not guilty. We can assume responsibility without incurring blame.

Likewise, the thrust of efforts to mitigate the continuing effects of past discrimination cannot lie solely in a search for illegal practices. Where we find people or organizations practicing discrimination we should of course demand corrective action. But that approach is of limited value in addressing the more general problem of substantive racial inequality. It treats one symptom of the problem, not the problem itself.

I have some general suggestions about how to proceed, but I offer a major caveat. What I have outlined in previous chapters represents theory. And theory is a long way from social policy. Before moving to policy we must know a lot more about how specific rules operate.

For example, the 1964 Civil Rights Act prescribes nondiscrimination in employment decisions and nondiscrimination in pay. It may well be that, in practice, the combination of those two aspects of the law produces perverse effects. The effects may be especially severe for economic marginals such as the unemployed black youth discussed in chapter 2. What we want to do is give employers incentives to hire economic marginals. When an employer is required to pay a high-risk applicant the same as he would pay a low-risk applicant, the choice may be fairly obvious, even absent a tendency to discriminate on grounds of race.

But before we have all the answers we must begin to address the problem of substantive racial inequality. We can do that, first, by making racial inequality a major policy issue. We must make it clear that this nation has a substantial interest in correcting the continuing effects of past racial injustice. And in conveying that message we may reject, as premature, questions about economic cost. In public policy, cost is usually the "but" that follows hard upon the "yes." Cost is not irrelevant. However, we should try to focus on the moral issue before we allow dreary accounting considerations to take center stage.

Second, we must stipulate a principle for public policy: no policy will be enacted that has a disequalizing effect. While we are trying to make things better we must ensure that they get no worse. For reasons that are not quite clear, the 1970s have seen some disequalization in the standing of blacks relative to whites—at least as regards income and unemployment. We must, very quickly, identify the factors that lead to these perverse effects, and seek to alter them.

As a matter of strategy, blacks should begin to form alliances with other groups trapped in the paradox of procedural equality. The groups that supported blacks during the struggle for equal treatment may not lend enthusiastic support to the struggle for substantive equality. But other large groups, notably Chicanos and Puerto Ricans, also suffer socioeconomic disadvantages heavily influenced by discrimination and its continuing effects. They, too, have a substantial interest in moving beyond rules that threaten to perpetuate their depressed status.

To the cause of substantive equality for categoric groups they bring the force of numbers. But they also bring intellectual power and moral leadership. Indeed, if we had to identify a moral successor to Martin Luther King, Jr., one of the leading candidates would be Cesar Chavez.

I have examined two sets of rules for distributing goods: rules of suffrage, which affect the distribution of political goods such as representation and legislative policy; and the rule of equal opportunity, which affects the distribution of economic goods. I have shown that the relationship between these rules and racial equality is open. From them, little follows about movement toward substantive equality. To the extent that those rules do allow inferences, the inferences must be pessimistic.

In chapter 3 I stipulated five conditions to be satisfied before we could claim that blacks and whites had equal political power. The first condition, the right to vote, was satisfied. The second condition, exercising the right, was satisfied only marginally. The third, securing representation in legislative bodies, is being satisfied as a result of recent changes in electoral rules, changes that decrease the ability of states to neutralize black votes. With this, blacks are in a position to influence the agendas of legislative bodies—the fourth condition.

However, a final condition, holding a winning legislative coalition, is not satisfied. Whenever black and white policy interests are diametrically opposed, blacks will lose. This outcome is mitigated by the fact that direct racial conflicts seldom emerge in legislative bodies. Further, there are situations in which blacks can use logrolling or depend upon the sympathy of whites to achieve winning coalitions. Indeed, only in these situations can blacks achieve the policy ends they desire. Blacks must depend upon whites to achieve their legislative ends; whites are not dependent on black support to the same degree. These facts will not support the claim that the races are equal politically.

These concerns would be less salient if blacks and whites had the same policy interests. But black and white opinions diverge on a number of issues, including measures intended to ensure economic security and nondiscrimination. My analysis of the relationship between the rule of equal opportunity and the distribution of economic goods suggests that blacks and whites may continue to hold modally different opinions on a wide range of public policy issues.

I am not optimistic that the rule of equal opportunity, as currently practiced, will serve to reduce substantive racial inequality. It is more accurate to describe the rule as weak, biased opportunity. It is designed to combat only one form of bias: discrimination. It does not address biases in the distribution of skills that result from past discrimination. Nor are there other rules or programs to attack other forms of bias systematically.

Further, the rule applies only to a portion of economic

goods. Even if it were to eliminate all bias, racial inequality might persist. At best, the relationship between the rule and substantive racial equality is open. There is no reason to believe that current rules will lead to racial equality, save for equality of rights.

To say that current inequality is the result of discrimination against blacks is to state only half the problem. The other half—the part generally not discussed—is discrimination in favor of whites. It follows that merely eliminating discrimination is insufficient. The very direction of bias must be reversed, at least temporarily. If we wish to eliminate substantive inequality we waste effort when we debate whether some form of special treatment for the disadvantaged group is necessary. What we must debate is how it can be accomplished.

Once we correct the problems created by past racial injustice we can begin to move toward a liberal society that places primary value on the individual, with rules that are indifferent to race or other categorical group identifications. But we cannot build a liberal political economy directly atop the smouldering debris of a racist society. To do so is to invite instability. Some of the new structures may stand, but others will suffer the stress of an uneven foundation.

One can pretend the stresses will go away, that cracks in the new structure are mere small accidents—unfortunate, unsightly perhaps, but inconsequential. One who thinks this way will settle for plastering a crack here, buttressing a wall there. But the problems lie deeper. We can try to ignore the basic structural defects and hope that in time all the pieces will settle into place. They will not.

Appendix

Open and Closed Rules

1. Closed rule: One that states or implies a substantive result. Given rule x, result y follows. Stated formally:

    a. If x, then y.

    b. If not-y, then not-x. That is, if the expected result does not occur, then the rule has been violated.

Thus a closed rule is one in which x is a *sufficient* condition for y to occur. But this does not mean that x is a *necessary* condition for y to occur. The result, y, could arise by other circumstances, including pure accident. Consider the two rules for dividing a cake equally. One is the closed rule, "All children will get equal pieces." The other is the open rule of cut-and-choose supplemented by the condition of rational egoism. Either of these will produce equal pieces of cake. And if equal pieces do not result we can infer that neither had been applied. But the result, equal pieces of cake, could occur even though neither the closed rule, nor the open rule plus condition, was applied. Equal pieces could result by inadvertence. A child could set out to divide the cake unevenly, but err. Therefore the following statements must contain qualifications:

    c. If y, then x,

        i. if y cannot result from causes other than x; or

        ii. if other possible causes of y have been eliminated or accounted for.

    d. If not-x, then not-y,

        i. unless y can result from other causes; or

        ii. unless other causes of y have been eliminated or accounted for.

These considerations will be important later, for example, when I consider the effects of discrimination and nondiscrimination. A preview: Consider a rule of nondiscrimination that says, "Pay group A as much as group B." This is a

closed rule with respect to the relative pay of *A* and *B*. I can infer that *A* and *B* will earn the same amount (per hour, per
piece, or per position); and if I find that they do not earn the
same amount I can infer that the rule has been violated. (If *x*,
then *y*; if not-*y*, then not-*x*.) The rule is sufficient to ensure a
result, equal wages.

But is it a necessary condition? That is, if I find that *A* and
B earn the same, can I thereby infer that a rule of nondiscrimination has been followed (if *y*, then *x*)? No.

Suppose a wage-competitive labor market in which employers, acting rationally, will hire the cheapest substitutable labor.
Suppose further an influx of immigrants who are obliged to
sell their labor more cheaply than native workers. Strictly
speaking, there exists discrimination in wages—a rule that prescribes that *A* be paid less than *B*. An economically rational
employer will choose to hire cheap immigrant labor. Native labor will have to choose between accepting lower wages and being replaced. In this way, initial discrimination in wages may
produce adjustments that, over time, result in rough wage
equality between immigrants and natives. Wage equality would
also result from a rule of nondiscrimination. So equal wages
could result from nondiscrimination or (under very narrow
conditions) discrimination. Deciding which rules had been followed would be a matter of empirical research.

2. Open rule: One that implies no substantive result. If *x*, then
x. If not-*x*, then not-*x*. Nothing else follows. Open rules apply
to rights or duties *only* as rights or duties. They imply nothing
about the distribution of substantive goods or about the actual
exercise of rights. An open rule, *x*, provides a necessary but not
a sufficient condition for a result, *y*.

3. A rule can be closed with respect to some results and open
with respect to others. For example, the rule for dividing cake
tells me about the distribution of the cake, but not about the
distribution of plates and forks.

Index

Yales Studies in Political Science

INVENTORY 1983